Interactions and Interventions
in Organizations

WILEY SERIES ON
INDIVIDUALS, GROUPS AND ORGANIZATIONS

Series Editor
Cary Cooper,
Department of Management Sciences,
University of Manchester Institute
  of Science & Technology,
Manchester

Associate Editor
Eric J. Miller,
Centre for Applied Social Research,
Tavistock Institute of
  Human Relations,
London

Theories of Group Processes
Edited by Cary Cooper,
University of Manchester Institute of Science & Technology

Task and Organization
Edited by Eric J. Miller,
The Tavistock Institute of Human Relations

**Creating a Community of Inquiry: Conflict,
Collaboration, Transformation**
William R. Torbert,
Graduate School of Education,
Harvard University

**Organizational Careers: Some
New Perspectives**
Edited by John Van Maanen,
Sloan School of Management,
Massachusetts Institute of Technology

**Interactions and Interventions
in Organizations**
Iain Mangham,
Centre for the Study of Organizational Change and Development,
University of Bath

Interactions and Interventions in Organizations

Iain Mangham
*Director, Centre for the Study of
Organizational Change and Development,
University of Bath*

JOHN WILEY & SONS
Chichester · New York · Brisbane · Toronto

Library of Congress Cataloging in Publication Data:

Mangham, I. L.
  Interactions and interventions in organizations.

  (Wiley series on individuals, groups, and
organizations)
  Bibliography: p.
  Includes index.
  1. Social interaction.   2. Organizational
change.   3. Organizational behavior. I. Title.
HM291.M369   301.18′32   78–2602

ISBN 0 471 99622 X

Photosetting by Thomson Press (India) Limited, New Delhi
and printed in Great Britain at the Pitman Press, Bath

For Olive, Catriona, and Alasdair

Acknowledgements

I would like to thank the following publishers for permission to use extracts in this book:

Oxford University Press, University of California Press, Free Press, Journal of Business, Journal of Applied Behavioural Science, Penguin, Little, Brown and Company, M.I.T Press, John Wiley and Sons, University of Alabama Press, Addison-Wesley, Harvard University Press, Jossey-Bass, Prentice-Hall, and Brooks Cole.

Contents

Editorial Foreword to the Series

Over the last decade, there has been an enormous growth of interest in the social and psychological aspects of institutional and organizational life. This has been reflected in a substantial upsurge in research and training in the field of organizational behaviour particularly in Institutes of Higher Education and Research throughout the Western World. Attention in this development has focused on the interrelationship between the individual, the variety of groups to which he belongs and the organizational environment within which he and his group operate.

The purpose of this series is to examine the social and psychological processes of these interrelationships, that is the nexus of individual/personal development, group processes and organizational behaviour and change. Within this context, a wide range of topics will be covered. These will include: the individual, his role and the organization; multiple roles and role conflict; the impact of group processes on personal and organizational development; strategies for 'humanizing' the organizational environment to meet individual and group needs; and the influence of technical and economic factors on organizational life.

The series will attempt to draw together the main schools of organizational behaviour including, for example, the American behavioural science tradition as reflected by Harvard, UCLA and National Training Laboratories, and the British socio-technical and open systems approaches of the Tavistock Institute of Human Relations. It is hoped that this will add significantly to understanding the distinctive characteristics of the various approaches and also provide a link between them through which individual, group and organizational behaviour can be seen in fuller perspective.

CARY COOPER
ERIC MILLER

Preface

I've been an organization tinker for about twenty years. I tinker for, and with, many types of organization: schools, prisons, universities, hospitals, armies, voluntary agencies, companies large and small, public and private. For the last ten years or so I've been fully employed tinkering. I even have an organization of my own which is exclusively devoted to tinkering with other organizations. The practice is habit-forming but quite legal; it's even encouraged. For me it started innocently enough, tinkering with groups of actors improvising plays, being amazed by what they developed and speculating about how it was that they accommodated, and were accommodated by, each other in the process of interaction. From such groups I moved into training groups and, almost imperceptibly, became addicted to tinkering with large-scale organizations.

The *Concise Oxford Dictionary* (1951) defines a tinker (among other things) as: 'a mender (especially itinerant), a rough-and-ready worker, a botcher, one who patches in an amateurish and clumsy fashion by way of repair or alteration'.

Organization tinkers patch, alter, and repair organizations in a rough-and-ready fashion. The practice has a long and honourable history as Petronius Arbiter (210 B.C.) indicates:

'We trained hard but it seemed that every time we were beginning to form up into teams, we would be re-organized. I was to learn later in life that we tend to meet any new situation by re-organizing: and a wonderful method it can be for creating an illusion of progress while producing confusion, inefficiency, and demoralisation!'

Frederick 'Speedy' Taylor attempted to give tinkering scientific status in the early years of this century, since when it has become a growth industry. Organizations are virtually beseiged by tinkers of one tribe or another: 'organization-and-methods' men, 'management-by-objective' men, 'organization-development' men. The tinker analogy is particularly appropriate to this latter group; it certainly applies to the work that I do and, judging by association and the literature, it applies with equal pertinence to the work of many of my colleagues.

Organization development consultants, like tinkers, may be thought of as somewhat romantic figures—slightly disreputable and plausible enough rogues existing on the fringes of respectable society, but epitomizing at the same time a kind of alternative, more bohemian, society. It is a stance which excites both envy and hostility in about equal measures.

Those of us who have been subjected to the 'it's-alright-for-you, you-don't-have-to-work-in-the-real-world' routine cannot doubt the envy our position generates. Equally there can be little doubt about the hostility that organization development creates among both managers and academics, the latter tending to be somewhat vituperative in their comments. Perrow (1972), for example, is heavily sarcastic in his views upon T-groups as a form of development:

'We should, then, bless T-Groups because they do for managers what pot, flower power, psychedelic experiences, encounter groups and hard-rock music do for the far-out younger generation. The search for spontaneity and authenticity should be never-ending, and if it must occur in the guise of better productivity in organizations, let it! The retrainees will return refreshed to the world of hierarchies, conflict, stupidity and brilliance, but the hierarchies are not likely to fade away.'

However, some of the hostility is not misplaced. Organization development men, like tinkers, are *sometimes* (please note the emphasis) plausible rogues. Some of them may be regarded as peddlers, hucksters, and quacks as well as tinkers. They are the tellers of tales, the weavers of spells. Using the language of democracy, of participation, of people and productivity, consensus and decision, they parley themselves into the hearts and minds of stern, upright businessmen. Much of the literature is couched in terms of sales pitches all too often replete with unsubstantiated claims for this or that nostrum, this or that form of development. Small wonder that the academic finds the field somewhat difficult to consider as a substantive body of knowledge!

However romantic, whatever tools he may carry in his knapsack, whatever his sales pitch the tinker is fundamentally a botcher, a patcher, and, in the pejorative sense of the word, an amateur. His approach is that of trial-and-error, suck-it-and-see. His tools are simple, his techniques crude and clumsy, his familiarity and understanding of his raw material relatively slight. To tinker with something is not to know what it is you are doing. By contrast, the master of his trade, the craftsman, far from patching, repairing, and altering in an amateurish or clumsy fashion is a professional, a confident, competent master of his tools, his techniques, and his materials. He *knows* what he is about, albeit intuitively; he *understands* how the parts fit together; he has a deep familiarity with his raw material and can be relied upon to utilize it in producing, time after time, finely wrought artefacts. The very notion of craftsmanship connotes excellence, properly finished work, skill and dexterity, aptness, fitness, and appropriateness; talent and resourcefulness, mastery and accomplishment; artistry, proficiency, and flair. It implies a consummate blend of knowledge and skill.

Few organization development consultants are craftsmen. Most of us are tinkers exhibiting some degree of skill but little artistry. Our practice runs well ahead of our understanding, so much so that when something 'works' we are often at a loss to know why. An all-too-familiar conference theme is: 'What is organization development? The more I do it, the less I understand it.' For the most part the activities we undertake in organizations consist of a number of techniques which have but a tenuous relationship with any systematic ideas about individuals, groups, organizations, or change. Our daily practice is surrounded by a cloud of unknowing, a mist of ignorance which, in our trade, can only be dispelled by appropriate theory and research.

Given this situation, some would prefer to remain tinkers. There is, as I have noted earlier in this preface, a strong streak of romanticism running through most organization development, often finding expression in aggressive, anti-intellectual, anti-science postures. The extreme adherents of such positions, however, deny the validity of thought, assert the primacy of feelings over reason, and consider that expression is far more important than understanding. They are sceptical and hostile towards words and numbers, theory and research.

Judging by the literature, such views are less in evid ›nce now than they were a few years ago. For the majority of writers, theorists ar.. practitioners alike, there is concern about the cloud of unknowing and the apparently aimless prosecution of techniques. Kurt Lewin's statement that 'there is nothing so practical as a good theory' now finds widespread approval and there is a growing recognition of the utility of models in the process of intervening. In the early days of organization development (less than fifteen years ago!) it could have been argued that theory outweighed practice, that the ideas of Kurt Lewin had but infrequently been put into practice. Today the balance is decisively the other way; the practice heavily outweighs the appropriate ideas. Given this state of affairs, where do we go from here?

In my view the problem is not that there is a shortage of ideas or a dearth of research. It is that the existing theoretical fragments and empirical generalizations are either not appropriate or not sufficiently integrated to provide a useful handle for the practitioners. Books and journals are full of ideas and research deriving from the so-called 'systems' perspective ('open', 'contingent', or whatever). Less in evidence but still significant are notions drawn from the humanistic perspective. The former tends to stress variables such as technology and the environment; the latter places emphasis upon the individual and his desires for self-actualization. In my estimation both approaches neglect that which ought to be the central concern of practitioners in organization development—interaction. We know precious little about the process of forming relationships and probably substantially less about the process of changing relationships within organizations. What is needed is more emphasis upon theory and research which is concerned with the fundamental process of social interaction, the central (and, all too often, taken-for-granted) feature of all social life within organizations or elsewhere. As Goldschmidt (1972) stresses: 'Social interaction is the very stuff of human life. The individuals of all societies move through life in terms of a continuous series of social interactions.'

This book provides such an emphasis. The reader will find little or no discussion of concepts such as task, technology, integration, differentiation, equifinality, systems, environment; what mention there is of these notions is couched in somewhat critical, occasionally downright hostile, language. The emphasis throughout is unashamedly upon persons, upon the interpretations they place upon the circumstances in which they find themselves, and upon the performances they construct in the light of their interpretations.

In Part I of the book I consider the need for an emphasis upon social interaction, give the background to my ideas, and present the framework which informs the rest of the book.

In Part II the application of the framework to organization is explored and in Part III the implications of the ideas for the practice of organizational analysis and development are considered.

The study of face-to-face interaction is not the province of any one discipline and the ideas presented in these pages are drawn from philosophers, sociologists, linguists, anthropologists, writers, dramatists, politicians, and psychologists. The resultant text is not a work of cognitive psychology, nor a primer in theory development or research methodology. It represents a drawing together of a number of ideas from different fields and a preliminary consideration of them from the point of view of myself in my activities as an organization development tinker who would wish to become a craftsman. My departure point has been Sapir's (1968) statement that society 'is being reanimated or creatively affirmed from day to day by particular acts of a communicative nature which obtain among individuals participating in it'. En route I have taken on board ideas from a host of others, Simmel (1950), Mead (1964), Blumer (1969), Burke (1962), Duncan (1968), McCall and Simmons (1966), Goffman (1959) to name but a few. I have not reached my destination, a thorough and integrated understanding of the processes of interaction and intervention, but I take consolation from the words of Robert Louis Stevenson: 'To travel hopefully is a better thing than to arrive, and the true success is to labour.'

My labour has been made bearable, even enjoyable, by a number of people: my friends and colleagues, Colin Eden, Stephen Fineman, John Mason, Adrian McLean, David Sims, and particularly Peter Reason who read and commented upon the draft at various stages but who should not be held responsible for its faults, by Cary Cooper who, as editor of the series, has encouraged me throughout, by graduate students who have not suffered my ramblings in silence, and by managers who wittingly and unwittingly have been the partners in my explorations.

To say that Pat Meadows prepared the manuscript cannot do justice to the effort she had expended on my behalf; she has worked through draft after draft with unfailing equanimity and considerable speed and accuracy for which I wish to record my gratitude.

The final acknowledgement must be to my family and friends who have provided me with the space, support, and energy to bring this project to fruition. My thanks to you all.

IAIN MANGHAM

PART I

Interactions

'Vladimir: It's the start that's difficult.
Estragon: You can start from anything.
Vladimir: Yes, but you have to decide.
Estragon: True.' (Beckett, 1956)

Chapter 1

Shouts, Assertions, and Disputations

In this chapter I will develop the argument that I briefly sketched in the introduction to this book: that the prevailing modes of explanation and the dominant modes of research in the literature and practice of organization development are derived largely from two sources, systems theory and humanism, and that such emphases are not appropriate to the development of the understanding of the practice of changing relations within organizations. I shall further put the case that the most fruitful approach is one deriving from the interactionist perspective.

Since time, space, tolerance, and energy are limited, some of what follows is neither logically set out nor closely argued. Some, indeed, is expressed in the form of a shout, a loud uproar in support of a particular position, or an exultation of a point rather than a detailed explication of it. Some, more restrained and with more obvious backing, has the character of assertion, and the rest is cast in the more recognizably academic form of almost mediaeval debate and argument which may be termed 'disputation'. I will begin with a series of assertions, but the reader is warned that for the most part the chapter will be punctuated with a mixture of sundry shouts and disputations.

A further word of caution is in order before we proceed. The terms '*systems*', '*humanism*', and '*interactionism*' are shapeless words. Like many such terms in social science there is little or no agreement as to their characteristics and some would even dispute the claim to a distinctive name for the ideas I am seeking to characterize. Still others, while accepting the need for distinctive names, will disagree strongly with my attempt to designate the features of the approaches. This, no doubt, will particularly be the case in my presentation and discussion of systems theory. In anticipation of such disputes and by way of defence, I must state unequivocally that my purpose is not to present a comprehensive or even fair review of systems theory or humanism (given that it were possible), but rather to highlight their problems in order to contrast them with my preferred alternative framework—social interactionism.

Systems Theory

I will begin, however, in the manner in which I do not intend to go on by attempting to be fair in outlining the characteristics of systems theory by reference to what I take to be an impeccable source, Buckley (1968), where the perspective is outlined as:

'A whole which functions as a whole by virtue of the interdependence of its parts is called a *system*, and the method which aims at discovering how this is brought about in the widest variety of systems has been called general systems theory. General systems theory seeks to classify systems by the way their components are *organized* (interrelated) and to derive "laws" or typical patterns of behaviour, for the different classes of systems singled out by the taxonomy.'

There can be no doubt that in the hands of people such as von Bertalanffy (1962), Buckley (1967), Ashby (1956), Allport (1960), and many others, general systems theory has been and continues to be a powerful tool for the analysis and understanding of behaviour at both micro and macro levels. In the hands of other less sophisticated behavioural scientists, however, the approach is in danger of trivializing the study of man, reducing the individual's status to that of being a 'product' of the forces which impinge upon him, or, still worse, to that of being a cog or a component in the giant machine called society.

The systems perspective, particularly in its deterministic emphasis, has passed directly into the literature of organizational analysis and development. It is the prevailing paradigm of many of those who speculate about organization and organization change. As Greenfield (1973) notes:

'Traditions dealing with organization as mechanisms or organisms usually find favour over those which, reflecting Weberian views, see organizations as complex patterns of choice made by individuals in pursuit of ends that are meaningful to them.'

Miles (1975) is reasonably representative of the prevailing tradition: for him organizations are entities which,

'. . . inseparably intertwine people and processes into what is currently referred to as a "socio-technical" system. People in organizations operate the technology, they run the process. But they, in turn, as part of the process, have much of their behaviour *determined* by the system they operate.' (Italics not in the original)

For Miles and, I would argue, for many others, systems theory is more concerned with factors, variables, and things rather than with individuals: 'The scholar is concerned with how these variables—goals, technology, and structure—relate to each other and how they serve, individually or jointly, as determinants of managerial behaviour and organizational performance.' He is, of course, sophisticated enough to acknowledge that such variables must be 'ultimately linked' with 'human variables' for complete explanation, but he considers it convenient to make use of these 'dimensions which are characteristics of organization as such, and not of the people within them'.

The ultimate linkage, acknowledged by Miles, is not simply a matter of crude constraint. True, Durkheim, whose ghost haunts many a naive systems theorist, argued that society controlled the individual by imposing constraints upon him through custom, law, and practice, reinforcing these constraints with punishment whenever appropriate. Parsons (1937), however, notes that in his later work Durkheim began to see that social rules do not 'merely regulate "externally" ' . . . they enter directly into the constitution of the actors' ends themselves'. This constraint or restraint becomes 'internal, psychological and self-imposed as well' (Wrong, 1961). The individual becomes part of the system responding unconsciously to the interplay of forces which surround him:

'Central to the natural system is the concept of homeostasis, or self-stabilization, which spontaneously, or naturally, governs the necessary relationships between parts and activities and thereby keeps the system viable in the face of disturbances stemming from the environment.' (Thompson, 1967)

Strauss (1976) notes with approval that organization development is becoming 'the systems approach it claims to be', notably in the moves towards organizational rather than 'attitudinal or small group variables'. He particularly approves of diagnoses and interventions in terms of organizational climate, technostructural, formal, and informal systems, and he sees the development of approaches based upon notions such as differentiation and integration, contingency theory, and 'the almost painfully structurally oriented' work of the Tavistock Institute as the salvation of organization development.

Strauss is decidedly not alone in his aspiration for the field. French and Bell (1973) see the concept of 'system' as 'a major assumption in organization development efforts' denoting 'the interdependency of components and an identifiable wholeness or Gestalt'. Margulies and Raia (1972) claim that 'Organizational Development is essentially a systems approach to the total set of functional and interpersonal role relationships in organizations'. For them, 'Planned organizational change, by its very nature, must consider the potential impact on *all* elements of the system when one of its elements or subsystems is changed'. Schmuck and Miles (1971) rely heavily on the systems concept in their work with schools, while Lippit (1971) is inclined 'to work upon the organization as a system or totality', and so is Kuriloff (1972), Schein (1965), Bennis *et al.* (1969), Beckhard (1969), Argyris (1971), Blake and Mouton (1969), and Lawrence and Lorsch (1969). The perspective reaches its apogee in the work of Alderfer (1976), who utilizes 'boundary permeability and relationship mutuality, two concepts from open systems theory, to explain steady and changing states of individuals, groups and organizations'.

Not only are explanations and understandings to be offered in systems terms; for many the whole basis of organization development itself may be conceived of in terms of the individual *versus* the organization. The facticity of organizations is taken for granted; it is assumed to be non-problematic. In a very similar posture to that adopted by Marxists (Nord, 1974), a number of writers and practitioners appear to see the individual as alienated by his organizations and/or his society and to see their own roles as 'helping people destroy' these organizations (Pages, 1974), or at least to 'come to terms' with them if organizations themselves cannot be redesigned to actualize values and reward interpersonal competence (Argyris, 1954). McGregor (1960) argued that a better fit might be attained under theory Y assumptions (people like to work, achieve, and be responsible) than under theory X assumptions (people prefer to be passive, dependent, and to be controlled). The last years of another founding father, Maslow (1971), appear to have been devoted to the struggle to reconcile the notion of self-actualization with what he saw as the organization's needs for structure, order, and consistency. Such views imply an entity that is the organization, the society—a system that is, that has being, and that moves in a wondrous way independently of its members to impose on, constrain, or coerce said members. Such a perspective is the 'world-taken-for-granted' of many of those who busy themselves trying to develop fulfilling, satisfying, or appropriate relationships between the organization and its members and between the organization and its environment.

The adoption of the systems perspective leads in many instances to a view of human behaviour as an expression of 'the bombardment of forces upon the individual'. From this perspective the human beings are not important, but the non-human, measurable variables assume great importance since it is these that constitute the bombardment. It is these factors that are internalized by the individual and which, it is assumed, control his behaviour. The search for these variables and their measurement is thus often taken to be the primary task of scholars and has led to a strong reliance upon positivistic approaches to research.

Positivism in social science may be characterized as depending upon the assertion that the concepts and methods employed in so-called natural science may be appropriately applied to form a 'science of man' or a 'natural science of society'. It rests upon the assumption that there are 'laws which govern human behaviour' and that these laws are discoverable by the application of the scientific method. Adoption of this viewpoint leads to a lack of concern for that which is not directly accessible—that which is not an 'object'. Behaviour is thus a suitable *object* or *fact* for analysis, but the mental processes which may create this behaviour are not. That which is worthy of study is that which may be approached by the 'scientific procedures' much favoured by Durkheim (1938), which

'. . . indicate first of all by what characteristic we might recognize the thing so designated, then classify its varieties, investigate by methodological induction what the causes of its variation are and finally compare these results in order to abstract a general formula.'

Positivism is strongly represented in research into organizations. Organization development academics, if not practitioners, regularly indulge in sharp bouts of self-flagellation during which they cry out, cast dust into the air, and shake their heads from side to side at the parlous state of research in this field. The more positivist the prescriptions, the greater the pain and the sharper the anguish. Kahn (1974) inflicts a severe beating (in this case upon others—not himself) and is particularly forceful and clear about the need for rigorous research as opposed to work that is 'concentrated on the experience of the trainees and change agents' (i.e. that which is of potential significance from an interactionist perspective). He regrets the absence of '*hard* criteria' and 'experimental treatment'. His prescription for a particular piece of research is worth quoting at length since both in its terminology and its principles it closely parallels the ideas of Durkheim spelled out in this chapter:

'It would be exciting to see an organizational development programme that included research designed to obtain separate estimates of the effects of identical substantive changes generated under participative and non-participative conditions. Such data could be provided, I think, by means of a design using "master" and "slave" groups. (I use the terms only in their figurative, mechanical sense). Workgroups would be chosen in sets of three, one in each set, randomly designated master, one slave, and one control. If one of the master groups decided in the course of an OD programme that the group should have the authority to set its own standards or choose its own methods of work and have access to current cost data, these same changes would be initiated in the slave group, but by conventional managerial instruction. An increase in productivity or satisfaction in the master groups, as compared to control groups, would be interpreted as the combined consequence of the participative experience and the substantive participative decisions. An increase in productivity or satisfaction in the slave groups, as compared to control groups, would be interpreted as the effect of the substance of the decisions without the motivational effect of participation. The difference in criterion changes in a master group as compared to the matched slave group would be interpreted as reflecting the effect of participation alone, the effects of decision content having been held constant experimentally with each such pair of groups.' (Reproduced by special permission from *The Journal of Applied Behavioral Science*. 'Organizational development; some problems and proposals', by Robert L. Kahn, Vol 10, No. 4, page 498. Copyright 1974 NTL Institute for Applied Behavioral Science.)

Such research is, by implication, to be welcomed, since in the eyes of its begetters it is true, important, rigorous, experimental, and elegant—in a word it is 'objective'. Strict compliance with the canons of objectivity guarantees rational enquiry which, in turn, is the basis of the development of a field of study.

Some Objections

The problems of systems theory, as I see them, are implied in much of the foregoing: its relative lack of concern with the individual actor, its consequent emphasis upon social facts external to the individual actor, and its heroic overuse of positivistic approaches to data collection.

The uncritical recourse to systems theory has tended to emphasize ideas of stability, interrelatedness, equilibrium, and integration. Its inherently conservative bias has led those directly involved with it to posit a view of man that is non-problematic: man internalizes the norms of his society and conforms. In Johnson's (1960) terms: 'Conformity to institutionalized norms is, of course, "normal". The actor having internalized the norms, feels something like a need to conform. His conscience would bother him if he did not.' For some systems theorists there is, apparently, little of concern in the relations between social norms, the individual's interpretation and selection of them, his subsequent behaviour, and his feelings about his action.

The picture that emerges is that of the individual actor completely moulded by the particular norms and values of his culture, a perspective which has extreme difficulty in accommodating ideas of change and deviance. It can, of course, be argued that the individual social actor does exist in a cultural milieu that is there in advance, is taken for granted, and is often passively received by consciousness. Alone or with others he behaves against this backcloth:

'. . . whether we happen to act alone or, cooperating with others, engage in common pursuits, the things and objects with which we are confronted as well as our plans and designs, finally the world as a whole, appear to us in the light of beliefs, opinions, conceptions, etc., that prevail in the community to which we belong.' (Gurwitsch, 1966)

It must not be assumed, however, that this process of assimilating the culture, this process of becoming human, necessarily implies a *standardization* of response. Social action must be understood in terms of the meanings particular social actors attach to their social world rather than as a product of an objectively defined set of conditions. There can be no certainty that a particular event will have a given meaning to all actors. Each social actor, as a consequence of innumerable successive involvements with other people and other events, will have developed an idiosyncratic approach—a way of interpreting and behaving, of ascribing meaning to the event—which is peculiar to himself and may not coincide with that of other actors.

The observation of behaviour in and of itself does not necessarily enable the observer to make sense of that behaviour. What the observer takes to be a simple physical action may imply totally different meanings to those concerned according to the way they each interpret the particular situation and circumstances. The meaning of a laugh, a scowl, a kick or a kiss is mediated by the actors involved in the event and has no meaning outside such mediation. It is not given for all time and all circumstances by the individual's culture, however apparently fixed such meanings may *appear* from time to time.

It is this aspect of the individual's mediation of his culture, the potential for non-conformity within us all, that many adopting the systems perspective tend to ignore. Systems men and women, particularly of the ilk that I have termed naive, are not concerned with ways of perceiving, with modes of thinking, nor with processes of planning and rehearsal of action. They have no interest in the forming, maintaining, or dissolving of relationships, processes which I shall argue are at the core of organization development.

From a research standpoint systems theory tends to emphasize the typical rather than the individual, to focus upon the main tendency of behaviour rather than the process of taking individual action. Its advocates are quite plain on this point, stressing that the central task of sociology, in the words of Tuman (1973), is that of showing 'why people behave as they do, by studying the influences of their group membership'. Hence the development of that which Blumer (1969) terms 'variable analysis': 'The conventional procedure is to identify something which is presumed to operate in group life and treat it as an independent variable, and then to select some form of group activity as the dependent variable.' The consequence of such approaches has been a heavy research emphasis upon identifying and measuring variables.

Such positivism in organizational research has ignored the possibility that human group activity is carried on, for the most part, through a process of interpretation and definition. Kahn's (1974) work, previously referred to, is undoubtedly guided by the rules, regulations, and norms which govern scientific objectivity. He is concerned with the operational definition of terms; he notes, for example, that 'Organization Development is not a concept, at least not in the scientific sense of the word; it is not precisely defined; it is not reducible to specific, uniform, observable behaviours'. Presumably he thinks that 'participation' may be so reduced and that 'productivity' and 'satisfaction' are likewise measurable concepts. Given this assumption, the rules of inference that he advocates are impeccably scientific. His subjects, the members of the 'master' and 'slave' groups, however, are not regarded as problematic. How they define the circumstances and how they consensually or individually interpret 'participation' is not considered to be an issue. The intervening process is ignored or, what amounts to the same thing, taken for granted as something that need not be considered.

The idea that the independent variable automatically exercises its influence upon the dependent variables, apparent though this may be in the physical sciences, is, a fallacy in the social sciences. The process of definition by the social actors involved appears to me to be absolutely crucial. Kahn's workers must define 'participation' for it to have any effect upon their productivity and their satisfaction. One group of workers may define participation as 'manipulation' and behave in a particular way while another group define it as 'freedom' and behave in a different way. The intervening interpretation is crucial to the outcome. It provides the meaning which sets the response and as such it should be necessary to incorporate it in the account of the research. Kahn's proposal, and the work of many others involved in research into organizations, assumes a fixity of meaning for the chosen variables which in most cases is unwarranted.

The tendency to ignore individual action in favour of a concentration upon the most frequent or most typical has a number of other implications. Such a research perspective tends to cast the individual social actor into the role of passive receiver of forces; in other words, the very nature of the research process which accompanies much of systems theory reinforces the basic tenets of systems theory. If individuals are to be seen as social products, as puppets rather than actors, research procedures cast in the positive format will tend to reinforce that view. Research will tend to be done *to* them or about them, but not with them, and, more importantly, such research will by its very nature confirm the image of man as a resultant of convergent social forces. A perspective and a research procedure which ignores the possibility that the individual can be the source of actions and strategies in his or her own life simultaneously denies such a possibility.

There is a danger that my critical remarks will be taken as implying that there is no value in either systems theory or in variable analysis. Further, they may be taken as implying that the one necessarily accompanies the other. On the contrary, I am in no doubt that the systems perspective is a useful one; it has illuminated and continues to illuminate many areas of social life that would otherwise remain obscure. Variable analysis is a fit and appropriate procedure for those areas of social and organizational life which are not mediated by processes of interpretation and definition. While useful and, in many cases, appropriate, neither systems theory nor positivistic variable analysis is sufficient to provide an intellectual framework for the practice of organization development. What is needed is an alternative or complementary conceptual scheme which acknowledges the central importance of the actor's interpretation of events and situations, and an alternative or complementary methodology which acknowledges the nature of research into social as opposed to physical reality and which is concerned with the qualitative rather than the quantitative aspects of that reality.

The Humanistic Perspective

The most popular alternative to systems theory, though nowhere as clearly articulated as a conceptual scheme, is the vague humanistic orientation which is evident in some of the organization development literature. The former tends to push organization development towards being more scientific, more theoretical and conceptual, more rigorous and quantitative; towards more abstract and generalizable models; towards an understanding of the determinants of social behaviour. Humanism, on the other hand, is less concerned with the building of concepts or models, less interested in diagnosis and planning, and more concerned with individual experience, individual choice, and individual acceptance. Much of this humanism derives from the training of organization development practitioners in experiential methods where the emphasis is often clearly upon personal experience and personal choice rather than upon conformity to general norms and forces.

As I have indicated, the scientific influence has led to an emphasis upon systems and upon positivism, and creates the idea that the scientist approaches organizational change and development with established concepts and models and is primarily, if not exclusively, concerned with deriving data to enrich his particular framework. Such data tend to be centred around things and abstracts rather than individuals and their experiences. The humanistic influence pushes organization development towards individuals, towards experience, towards intuition and subjectivity. Each operates from and promotes a different image of man. That which I have characterized as systems theory with its emphasis upon the search for determinants of behaviour conceives of man as a rational being whose mind is originally void of any structure but which receives and acts upon the impressions of environmental structure. Humanism is its polar opposite since the image of the individual which informs its approach is that of the individual at the centre of events, the creator rather than the responder. The beginnings of the humanistic doctrine may be traced to the statement by Protagoras in 400 BC: 'Man is the measure of all things, of things that are that they are, and of things that are not that they are not.' This philosophy or set of assumptions clearly rejects objectivity and equally clearly disavows environmental determinism.

Solomon (1971) argues that the applied behavioural scientist is 'an actualizer of values'. In his work with his clients his job is to bring about change in the direction of the 'desired' or 'desirable' values—that which is 'desired' often being given by the client, such as 'increased profit, lower employee turnover', etc., and that which is 'desirable', such as the release of the individual's creative energy, being derived from the theoretical framework upon which the consultant's skills are based. He goes on to argue that humanism, the philosophy which accords centrality to man, provides a firm value base for interventionists.

Tannenbaum and Davis (1969) are equally concerned about the question of values and, like Solomon, they consider humanism to be the appropriate framework for organizational development academicians and practitioners. Unlike Solomon, they do consider that such people are generally aware of the humanistic perspective and that such values are shared. Indeed, they claim that humanism, in one form or another, is the most 'pervasive common characteristic among people in laboratory training and in organizational development', though it may not be as explicitly stated as it might be.

The values enumerated by Tannenbaum and Davis (1969) very clearly deal with individuals and persons rather than inputs and organisms. In much of what they write they appear to be echoing the words of Maslow (Buhler and Allen, 1972): 'I must approach a person as an individual, unique and peculiar, as the sole member of his class', and of Kelly (1970): 'We start with a *person*. Organisms, lower animals, and societies can wait. We are talking about someone we know, or would like to know—such as you, or myself. More particularly, we are talking about this person as an event—the processes that express his personality. . . .'

Humanism clearly and unequivocally rejects environmental determinism; Adler (1956) asks the question and answers it: 'Who seeks, who answers, who utilizes the impressions from the environment? Is man a dictaphone or a machine? There must be something else at play.'

For the humanist the appropriate model for the analysis of social behaviour is anthropomorphic. Unlike the cruder forms of systems theory, there is no attempt to use the analogue of the machine, the hydraulic system, or the organism; the human being must look to other humans as its own model. Furthermore, the perspective involves an acknowledgement that we are dealing with unique individuals and with whole persons who cannot (or should not) be subdivided into drives or motives. As Matson (1971) puts it, the common denominator of the various schools of humanistic thought is

'. . . respect for the person, recognition of the other not as a case, or an object, or a field of forces, or a bundle of instincts, but as himself. . . . This recognition of man-in-person, as opposed to man-in-general, goes to the heart of the difference between humanistic psychology . . . and scientific psychologies such as behaviourism.'

Another basic assumption of the humanistic approach is that a human being is a process and, as such, continually changing and developing. Tannenbaum and Davis (1969) put the issue cogently when they comment that the traditional view of individuals is that they are to be defined in terms of given traits, skills, and personality characteristics, all of which are relatively enduring: 'This view, when buttressed by related organizational attitudes and modes, ensures a relative fixity of individuals, with crippling effects. The value to which we hold is that people can constantly be in flux, groping, questing, testing, experimenting, and growing.'

Humanistic man grows and 'develops to be what he makes himself by his own actions' (Langer, 1969); a key phrase, on the lips of many humanistic theorists, deriving from the work of Maslow (1970), is 'self-actualization and self-fulfilment'. The person strives to make of himself that which is truly fulfilling. As an active seeker of stimuli, as a reflective being, as an experiencer of life subjectively as it takes place, the person grows into a fully functioning human being. Being aware and being reflective, the person becomes the mediator of his own experiences and the shaper of his own self-concept. Being at the centre of the world, the individual is responsible for his own behaviour, is purposive, and is accountable for his actions.

This emphasis upon the human person, upon the individual, his experiences, and his choices, is the central feature of the humanistic approach. But there is an important corollary without which the assumptions about humanistic man would be incomplete and unfairly distorted. A number of writers who may be broadly lumped together as being of a humanistic orientation emphasize the importance of relationships to the development of the self and hence the stress in much of their writings on theories of dialogue, confrontation, encounter, meeting, intersubjectivity, and so on.

Buber's work is probably the most influential and his concept of the 'I–Thou' relation has been well described by Herberg (1956):

'The term I–Thou points to a relation of person to person, of subject to subject, a relation of reciprocity involving "meeting" or "encounter", while the term I–it points to a relation of person to thing, of subject to object, involving some form of utilization, domination, or control, even if it is only so-called "objective" knowing.'

The fully functioning human being has the capacity and the will to initiate interaction with others, to reach out to them, and to share his experiences and himself with others, and in so doing can come to a fuller understanding of himself. 'The fact is,' writes Marcel (1960), 'that we can understand ourselves by starting from the other, or from others, and only by starting from them, . . . it is only in this perspective that a legitimate love of self can be conceived.'

The shortcomings of a naive systems perspective have been well rehearsed in these pages and elsewhere and do not need to be repeated here. The humanistic image of man, while, perhaps, more superficially attractive in that it accords centrality to the person, likewise has a number of shortcomings. It has led to a denial of the impact of society upon the individual and a curious kind of anti-intellectualism nourished by an overemphasis upon feelings, upon phenomenology, and upon the idiosyncratic as the only basis for true knowledge.

Naive humanism is almost as narrow and certainly as restrictive in its view of the individual as is naive systems thinking. Despite the contributions of people such as Buber, humanism tends to place a heavy emphasis upon the single individual. Many of its basic tenets constitute nothing more than a hymn to individual freedom, a celebration of personal growth and development. At its most naive—or most fundamental, depending upon your point of view—it proposes the worship of feelings rather than the praise of reason. When humanists 'feel' they really feel; they 'let it all hang out' in the belief that emotional release is the key to creativity and self-actualization. The choice of words such as 'worship' and 'belief' to describe the articles of faith (there is another such term) is quite deliberate on my part since to many of the non-elect such as myself, humanists appear to subscribe to a form of religious movement marked by strange rituals and incantations. Almost anything can be, and has been, justified in the cause of deep, individual feeling.

Such a focus on the single individual with little or no acknowledgement of the dialectical interplay between the self and others leads to a denial of the possibility of generalization and, hence, to a hostility towards research methods which seek to discover general laws. Not surprisingly, little research is attempted by naive humanists and little theory is either developed or read, since emotions are to be experienced, not described. Little thought is given to the discovery of concepts or the propagation of ideas, since thinking is itself considered less important than being. Humanists produce little in the way of thought or research into organizations, presumably since many are much more concerned with the development of alternative life-styles rather than with the problems of relations within contemporary organizations.

If the systems perspective becomes little more than a reification of the forces which impinge upon the individual in the hands of its less sophisticated adherents, naive humanism becomes little more than the worship of the freak and the drop out, leading only to a crude emotional narcissism.

Whatever the strengths and weaknesses of the two perspectives, neither, it seems to me, does justice to the complex interrelationship of man, society, and communication. In essence systems man is determined, humanistic man is the determiner. While there is some acknowledgement within each tradition that such views are simplistic and partial (Ansbacher, 1971; Miles, 1975), nonetheless the overall impression that remains is that of man as either automaton or artist, slave or bohemian. But man may be conceived of as both automaton *and* artist, slave *and* bohemian; determined *and* determiner.

What is needed is a perspective which does justice to both concepts, a perspective which not only acknowledges that man is shaped by Destiny but also shapes his own destiny. Such a framework may be derived from the work of writers such as Max Weber and George Herbert Mead.

Social Interactionism

According to Weber (1947) the task of sociology is to understand 'social action' which is defined as:

'In action is included all human behaviour when and insofar as the acting individual attaches a subjective meaning to it. (Action is) social insofar as by virtue of the subjective meaning attached to it by the acting individual (or individuals) it takes account of the behaviour of others and is thereby oriented in its course.'

Action is oriented by the account the actor takes of the other; the actor is aware of the other and adjusts his conduct accordingly. It will be clear from the quotation that the ghost of Max Weber has haunted this book from the first page and will continue to do so for much of that which follows. However, the substance of the alternative conceptual scheme I am proposing derives much more directly from George Herbert Mead. Weber was not particularly interested in addressing himself to the issue of how the individual actor takes account of the behaviour of others; Mead and his followers have devoted some considerable effort to this, and it is to them that I will turn for the broad background to my ideas.

Mead argues that the characteristic that distinguishes man from other animals is his capacity for symbolic representation and symbol manipulation. Man, as a social actor, can take account of the present in the light of his past experience and the anticipated future through the medium of symbols. By reference to such symbolic representations of past and future states he can, and does, orient his behaviour. Unlike matter, he does not simply behave in response to a stimuli; he constructs a meaning for that with which he is confronted and behaves in accordance with the meaning so ascribed. This is the first of the basic premises of 'symbolic interactionism'. Human beings act towards things on the basis of the meanings that the things have for them. The second premise is that these meanings are themselves the products of social interaction in human society. The meanings of particular events, situations, things, and experiences arise out of the observed behaviour of significant others towards them. The meaning of the office or role of managing director, for example, is given by the way people behave towards that role or function: reverentially, subserviently, or whatever. The third premise holds that these meanings are modified and handled by an interpretive process that is used by each individual in dealing with the situations he or she encounters. Given my particular set of experiences I may ascribe a different meaning to the role of the managing director and behave accordingly, behaviour which, in turn, may modify the interpretations of others and thus affect their behaviour which influences my interpretation, and so on.

From this perspective the individual assumes an importance lacking in much of systems theory. Human beings are defined as the *actors*, the initiators of action, and not simply as those acted upon, the responders. They are defined as organisms with selves which construct, direct, and monitor behaviour. Unlike 'humanistic man' they are not to be seen as entirely self-willed creatures driven by forces within them:

'The behaviour of men and women is "caused" not so much by forces within themselves (instincts, drives, needs, etc.) or by external forces impinging upon them (social forces, etc.), but what lies in between, a reflective and socially derived interpretation of the internal and external stimuli that are present.' (Meltzer, Petras, and Reynolds, 1975)

From this perspective the social actor can be seen to exist in dual systems. He is both influenced by and influences the social order which he inhabits. I am influenced by the repertoire of meanings and behaviour which have accrued around the office of managing director, but I also can influence and extend the repertoire either by accident, ignorance, or design. Given this, the social order may be considered to be no more important than the individual who creates it, interprets it, and responds to it. The influence of variables external to the individual is only capable of being experienced in terms of the social meanings attributed to them by individuals, and such attributions are learned in social interaction. Thus, in Meltzer, Petras, and Reynolds' (1975) terms, 'behaviour is constructed and circular, not predetermined and released'.

Qualitative Research

The research methodology appropriate to such a perspective upon human action is, of course, not that of positivism with its emphasis upon the average and, all too often, its heavy reliance on statistical inference about concepts which have an indefinite relation to the empirical world. Positivism, at least in the form I am criticizing, has tended to stand off from its potential subject matter; conversely, an appropriate research methodology, *qualitative research*, manifests a close association with human action. An empirical science is not to be brought into being by endless debate and disputation about concepts with the weakest of empirical referents; it is constructed out of the interplay of data and speculation that generates the concepts and at the same time *grounds* them in a context of empirical materials. Blumer (1969) puts it with his usual clarity:

'Most of the improper use of the concept in science comes when the concept is set apart from the world of experience, when it is divided from the perception from which it has arisen and with which it ordinarily ties. Detached from the experience which brought it into existence, it is almost certain to become indefinite and metaphysical. I have always admired a famous statement of Kant which really defines the character of the concept and indicates its limitations. Kant said brilliantly: "Perception without conception is blind; conception without perception is empty".' (Herbert Blumer, *Symbolic Interactionism: Perspective and Method*, © 1969. By permission of Prentice-Hall, Inc., Englewood Cliffs, New Jersey.)

The way to avoid emptiness and to stimulate groundedness is to be intimately familiar with one's subject matter—to have a detailed and dense awareness of a particular set of social actors over a period of time and to seek to understand how it is that they go about defining and acting in their particular social world; to participate with them while observing or, as a second best, to spend a considerable amount of time talking to them in a relatively unstructured form about their perceptions and their actions.

In this respect many organization development practitioners may be surprised to find that, like Moliere's character who discovered he had been talking prose all of his life, they have been practising qualitative research all of their lives. Participation, immersion, and deep familiarity with a particular set of social actors in specific circumstances, however, while a necessary condition, is not a sufficient one for the development of a research tradition. Qualitative research, if it is to develop, needs to go beyond the case study, beyond the mere collection of data and the accumulation of experiences. A qualitative research programme needs to be able to link the specific with the general and to delineate the particular in terms of its universal, transcendent, and analytic aspects. To do this, working from the observed situation or from the perceptions of those involved in that situation, the qualitative researcher should be able to draw out a number of inferences which have wider application and to present these inferences at an appropriate level of abstraction. The best work in this developing tradition presents both concepts and the concrete instances which embody or illustrate them. Within the field of organizational development the work of Dalton (1970) on the processes of organizational change and of Argyris (1970) on intervention come down to the kind of qualitative approaches I have in mind. Such examples, however, are as yet rare in the literature. Much of what is claimed as research consists of (1) little more than the forcing of new data into pre-established categories or existing theoretical frameworks, (2) abstract ramblings about concepts such as values divorced from any empirical referent, or (3) detailed accounts of particular interventions with little or no attempts at generalization. Qualitative research is based upon the conviction that knowledge is most effectively promoted by a close interplay between the abstract and the concrete. Too much abstraction carries with it the danger of empty speculation, too much concreteness the possibility of blind floundering in a morass of data. Qualitative research seeks to redress or to avoid some of the problems of positivism while at the same time not denying the rigour essential to the development and accumulation of ideas. In Reason's (1976) terms it is *holistic* in the sense that its practitioners seek to immerse themselves in the stream of experience and understand it as a totality rather than as a series of separate, manipulatable variables. The would-be qualitative researcher begins by discovering what it is that his coparticipants are doing, feeling, thinking, and experiencing; the actual experience as it occurs is the starting point, from which 'buzzing, blooming confusion' the researcher seeks to draw out and articulate the concepts which capture the experience. Such an approach raises all sorts of issues about researcher/client relationships about which it is not appropriate to speculate here, but it does, in its very proximity to its material and its reluctance to impose concepts upon it, represent a significant alternative to the more familiar positivistic approaches.

Social interactionism provides the basis of a theoretical perspective for those engaged in organization development; qualitative research gives a perspective on the nature of the appropriate method for generating knowledge in the area. The two approaches are both complementary and congruent. The activist image of human conduct that suffuses much of social interactionism, the central position it accords to the individual social actor, fits well with emphasis of qualitative research upon the understanding of the concrete experience of individuals as they participate in social situations.

Summary

Kahn's prescription for research and the ideas of those organizational theorists most frequently cited with approval by organization development practitioners, 'March & Simon, Blake & Mouton, Coch & French, Lawrence & Lorsch, Morse & Reiner, Trist & Bamforth, Katz & Kahn, Drucker & James Thompson' (Weisbord, 1974), reveal that many have forgotten that they are dealing with *human* organizations. Such prescriptions reveal a marked tendency to conceive of organizations as creations apart from people, as entities capable of having goals, responding to the environment and controlling and processing people. Thompson (1967), arguably one of the most influential organizational theorists, appears to hold to the conception of the individual as little more than an 'input':

'. . . if the modern society is to be viable it must sort individuals in to occupational categories, equip them with relevant aspirations, beliefs, and standards; and channel them to relevant sectors of the labor market'.

Much organization theory is of the same ilk; it treats the 'human factor' as an input or, somewhat less starkly, the individual as an organism. Such terms imply a sameness of individuals and are thus considered to be appropriately objective and scientific in that they may be used to predict normative behaviour. Such terminology also leads to a tendency to downplay or ignore both the idiosyncratic and the more human aspects of man's behaviour: his peculiar attributes of using language, attributing meaning, and monitoring his own behaviour, facilities he does not share with other 'inputs' or 'organisms'.

So we have an image of man as an organism, environmentally determined and adapting to his environment, be that his immediate fellows or society in general, through a process of socialization. Behaviour occurs as a result of forces in the environment acting upon the individual. From this perspective, the individual organism is nothing but a passive, blank mind endowed with only one ability, that of being activated by external stimuli. A further assumption is that since the organism will tend to do that which is reinforced, it operates on hedonistic principles. Systems man seeks pleasure and avoids pain and is thus readily socialized. Systems man is also seen to be a conditioned creature who will behave relatively predictably being, as he is, little more than a reflection of the environment. The human being is an organism whose mental processes are merely the associations between stimulus and response or the 'throughput' from 'input' to 'output'.

In marked contrast, the humanistic image of man stresses his 'freedom of the mind and the autonomy of the person . . .' and much of humanism is devoted to 'exposing and condemning each and every dehumanizing, depersonalizing and demoralizing force' (Matson, 1969). Some of the writing and of the therapeutic practice deriving from humanism and existentalism is seen even by its adherents to be marked by a strong sense of irresponsibility. Matson (1969) sees humanistic psychology as having become 'a haven for the irrational and the anti-intellectual—for all that is exotic, erotic and psychotic'. In a similar vein Maslow (1970) wrote: 'I share with many other scholars and scientists a great uneasiness over some trends in Esalen-type education. For instance in some of the less respectworthy adherents, I see trends toward anti-intellectualism, anti-science, anti-rationality, anti-discipline, anti-hard work, etc. . . .' Despite the efforts of a great many writers to stress that the individual is socially embedded, the tenor of humanism has been one of individual independence—'doing your own thing'—rather than of interdependence and cooperation, and such research as has been prosecuted in this tradition has been necessarily idiographic rather than nomethetic.

Social interactionism avoids the excesses of naive systems theory and humanism and stresses the interrelationship of the person and the society of which he is a part. The individual is seen as existing in dual systems—what Mead (1956) referred to as sociality; there is a reciprocity missing from both systems theory and humanism in that it is the person who creates or sustains the influences to which he is to some degree subject. From this perspective, organizations are to be understood in terms of the individuals who participate in them and individuals are to be understood in terms of the organizations of which they are members. Such 'understanding' can only arise from an intimate familiarity with the processes occurring within organizations, a familiarity which is at the heart of qualitative research which aims to go beyond the idiographic without doing violence to the complexity of its subject matter. Familiarity, it may safely be said, breeds concepts.

Chapter **2**

Totus Mundus Agit Histrionem

In this chapter I shall present my '*root metaphor*', that of the social world as theatre, and seek to give it substance by reference to a limited number of writers who have adopted a similar perspective. The need to have recourse to extensive quotes and to state the obvious creates a condition where the reader already familiar with the concept of life as drama is advised to turn to the end of the chapter for a summary of my views. For those less well read there is little choice but to grin and bear it.

At the beginning of the previous chapter I pointed out that the concept of 'interactionism' like that of 'systems' was a somewhat shapeless term. The subsequent discussion may have obscured the point, but the issue remains since it is difficult to define and almost impossible to secure agreement on what constitutes interactionism as a theoretical perspective beyond the basic premises outlined above. Some commentators see two major schools of thought within the broad framework, some as many as ten. Inevitably the distinctions are fine and themselves open to dispute.

My perspective, while eclectically derived from a number of the varieties, is primarily that of the 'dramaturgical school' and, as such, involves a very clear choice of metaphors. The idea of social life as theatre may draw attention to important properties of social existence but it does so only by way of analogy, and the pursuit of a particular analogy represents a choice which may block perceptions of features more readily accessible through the use of alternative analogies. The relentless pursuit of a single analogy, be that of society as a machine, an organism, or a theatrical arena, may be misleading. Nonetheless, the choice of metaphor or analogy appears to be inevitable:

'Metaphor is, at its simplest, a way of proceeding from the known to the unknown. It is a way of cognition in which the identifying qualities of one thing are transferred in an instantaneous, almost unconscious, flash of insight to some other thing that is, by remoteness or complexity, unknown to us.' (Nisbet, 1969)

Drama is my *root metaphor*; a concept delineated most clearly by Pepper (1942):

'The method in principle appears to be this: A man desiring to understand the world looks about for a clue to its comprehension. He pitches upon some idea of common-sense fact and tries if he cannot understand others areas in terms of this one. The original area then becomes his *basic analogy* or *root metaphor*. He describes as best he can the characteristics of this area, or if you will, "discriminates its structure". A list of its structural characteristics becomes his basic concepts of exploration and description. We call them a set of categories. . . . In terms of these categories he proceeds to study all other areas of fact . . . he undertakes to interpret all facts in terms of these categories. As a result of the impact of these other facts upon his categories, he may qualify and readjust the categories so that a set of categories continually changes and develops. Since the basic analogy or root metaphor normally (and probably at least in part necessarily) arises out of common sense, a great deal of development and refinement of a set of categories is required if they are to prove adequate for a hypothesis of unlimited scope. Some root metaphors prove more fruitful than others, have greater power of expansion and adjustment. These survive in comparison with others and generate relatively adequate world theories.' (Copyright © 1970 by The Regents of the University of California; reprinted by permission of the University of California Press.)

Clearly the 'systems' metaphor favoured by many is one that has survived the test of expansion, adequacy, and adjustment and has proved useful in the analysis of social life. Nonetheless, as I have indicated, there are dangers in invoking the metaphor, particularly in its more mechanistic forms. The use of any metaphor may mislead us about the nature of the human social world, *sui generis* unless the metaphor is itself derived from human life. The proper analogy for man is man. The appropriate metaphor is one that reflects the behaviour of conscious, volitional agents or actors, that acknowledges that man inhabits a cultural world rather than a natural or mechanical system. Life as drama is such a metaphor. It holds that the social world is capable of conceptualization in terms of the stage, that social reality is realized theatrically, that life is theatre, and that action is inherently dramatic.

The metaphor clearly passes Pepper's survival test. The part played by it as a compelling image in literature goes back thousands of years. Plato used it and it was a commonplace by the sixteenth century throughout Europe. Cervantes acknowledges this when he allows Sancho to deflate Don Quixote's use of it:

'Tell me, have you not seen some comedy in which kings, emperors, pontiffs, knights, ladies, and numerous other characters are introduced? One plays the ruffian, another the cheat, this one a merchant and that one a soldier.

Yet when the play is over and they have taken off their players' garments, all the actors once more are equal.

"Yes," replied Sancho, "I have seen all that."

"Well," continued Don Quixote, "the same thing happens in the comedy and intercourse of this world, where some play the part of the emperors, others that of pontiffs—in short, all the characters that a drama may have—but when it is all over, that is to say, when life is done, death takes from each the garb that differentiates him, and all at last are equal in the grave."

"It is a fine comparison," Sancho admitted, "though not so new but that I have heard it many times before. . . ."

Shakespeare's use of the analogy passes the test of expansion, adjustment, and adequacy. He transformed it from a simple allegorical figure 'into a complex imaginative mode of expression':

'Gradually the association of the world with the stage, fundamental to Elizabethan drama, built itself deeply into his imagination, and with the structure of his plays. . . . In his hands something individual and characteristically brilliant emerged from a theatrical commonplace of the age.' (Righter, 1962).

Such has been the power of the analogy that the 'theatrical commonplace' is now an everyday commonplace. The image of the world as theatre is readily apparent in references to the 'performances' of others, in comments about 'overacting' and 'underplaying', in the attribution of 'character' and 'role' to self and others, and the references to 'scenes', 'sets', 'cues', 'audiences', and 'stages'. The commonplace is of the world itself as a place where we each play out parts in the cosmic drama.

The Use of the Analogy by Social Scientists

Given the kind of pedigree, the antiquity, and the ubiquity of the commonplace, it is surprising to find that it has been openly adopted by only a few social scientists. Perhaps it is the pervasiveness of the analogy which has led to its disregard by the majority though, no doubt, the power of newer analogies more manifestly scientific has much to do with the neglect.

At its simplest it is openly acknowledged to be a metaphor and is pursued in functional and/or positivistic terminology. Biddle and Thomas (1966) are most representative of this point of view and are worth quoting at length:

'The role perspective consists of a particular viewpoint regarding those factors presumed to be influential in governing known behaviour, and it may best be introduced by resorting again to a theatrical analogy.

When actors portray a character in a play, their performance is determined by the script, the director's instructions, the performances of fellow actors, the reactions of the audience as well as by the acting talents of the players. Apart from differences between actors in the interpretation of their parts, the performance of each actor is programmed by all of these external factors: consequently, there are significant similarities in the performances of actors taking the same part, no matter who the actors are.

Now let us take this analogy into real life, using some of the terms of role theory. Individuals in society occupy positions, and their role performance in these positions is determined by social norms, demands and rules; by the role performances of others in their respective positions; by those who observe and react to the performance; and by the individual's particular capabilities and personality. The social script may be as constraining as that of a play but it frequently allows more options: the "director" is often present in real life, as in the play, as a supervisor, parent, teacher, or coach; the "audience" in life consists of all those who observe the position member's behaviour; the position member's "performance" in life, as in the play, is attributable to his familiarity with the "part", his personality and personal history in general, and more significantly, to the "script" which others define in so many ways. In essence, the role perspective assumes, as does the theatre, that performance results from the social prescriptions and behaviour of others, and that individual variations in performance, to the extent that they do occur, are expressed within the framework created by these factors.' (Reproduced by permission of John Wiley and Sons, Inc.)

The use of the metaphor in this way has a long history and is relatively common among social scientists, whether they are aware of the source of the analogy or not. Parsons, Merton, Gross, Linton, Allport, and a host of others all have recourse to the role concept in explicating their theories, and each of them defines role in essentially functional terms. Role performance, for many of them, is seen to consist of an actor *conforming* behaviourally to expectations communicated to them by others. Katz and Kahn (1966) are equally deterministic in their use of the analogy to refer to behaviour within organizations mixing both systems and theatrical ideas:

'Generically, role behaviour refers to the recurring action of an individual, appropriately interrelated with the repetitive activities of others so as to yield a predictable outcome. The set of interdependent behaviours comprise a social system or subsystem, a stable collective pattern in which people play their parts. . . . Moreover, in formal organizations the roles people play are *more a function of the social setting than of their own personality characteristics*.' (Italics mine) (Reproduced by permission of John Wiley and Sons, Inc.)

For them the basic criterion for studying behaviour within organizations is to ascertain the 'role expectations of a given set of related offices, since such expectations are one of the main elements in mentioning the role system and *inducing the required role behaviour*' (italics mine).

Writers such as McCall and Simmons (1966) and Goffman (1959) use the analogy in a much less deterministic fashion. The former explicitly challenge the functional perspective of role theory and of Parsons, Merton, and Gross in particular:

'In our opinion the sort of mechanistic conformity to a role script is observed only in consensual circumstances, as in fairly tightly structured organizations in which roles in this sense are formally defined. Even then the utility of the model is highly limited. Although the professor and the groundkeeper both occupy roles in the same formal organization, the professor would be at a loss to specify the role relationship between them in terms of specific expectations, rights and duties. We submit that no script exists for this role relationship, as indeed for the great majority of relationships, and therefore that the individuals involved must somehow improvize their roles within very broad limits. To the role theorist, the archetypical role is that seen in ritual or classic drama in which every line and every gesture of every actor is rigidly specified in the sacred script. In our view, the archetypical role is more nearly that seen in improvized theatre, such as is provided by the Second City Troupe, which performs extemporaneously within only the broad outlines of the sketches and of the characters assumed.' (Copyright © 1966. Reproduced from G. J. McCall and J. L. Simmons, *Identities and Interactions*, by permission of MacMillan Publishing Co., Inc.)

Goffman is even more firmly concerned with the individual social actor and his capacity to 'manage' the impressions others receive of him. He argues that each actor 'performs' or puts on a 'show' for the other and that in so doing he utilizes 'routines', 'parts', 'settings', and 'props'. Goffman's (1959) approach is openly theatrical:

'The perspective employed in this report is that of the theatrical performance; the principles derived are dramaturgical ones. I shall consider the way in which the individual . . . presents himself and his activity to others, the ways in which he guides and controls the impressions they form of him, and the kinds of things he may and may not do while sustaining his performance before them.'

Far from the individual's action being determined or controlled by the situation or circumstance in which he finds himself, Goffman's social actor seeks to determine and control:

'This control is achieved largely by influencing the definition of the situation which the others care to formulate, and he can influence this definition by expressing himself in such a way as to give them the kind of impression that will lead them to act voluntarily in accordance with his own plan.'

The outcome of each performance is an imputation by the target audience of a particular role or, more fundamentally, a particular kind of self to the performer. This imputation is as much, if not more, a result of the form of the actor's behaviour rather than its substantive element. Goffman captures this aspect most clearly in the following passage:

'. . . All of these general characteristics of performances can be seen as interaction constraints which play upon the individual and transform his activities into performances. Instead of merely doing his task and giving vent to his feelings, he will express the doing of his task and acceptably convey his feelings.'

In sharp contrast to the image of man implied by systems theory, Goffman's image of man implies an active, participating being who tries to fathom out what others are up to and accordingly manages the impressions he wishes to convey, primarily for the purpose of controlling their behaviour and achieving his own objective. The approach, with its clear emphasis on the calculative, manipulative, and situational behaviour of *actors*, reinforces the general interactionist view that norms, values, structures, and roles are simply the framework or settings within which interaction occurs.

Despite his heavy reliance upon theatrical or dramaturgical concepts, Goffman does not lose sight of the fact that he is doing nothing more than exploiting a particular analogy. In the final pages of his most influential book, *The Presentation of Self in Everyday Life* (1959), he drops the language of the stage and takes down his analogical scaffold:

'Now it should be admitted that this attempt to press a mere analogy so far was in fact a rhetoric and a manoeuvre.'

Similarly, Biddle and Thomas (1966) and McCall and Simmons (1966) see the ideas they utilize as 'mere analogies' not to be pressed too far since such devotion to a thoroughgoing metaphorical conceptual scheme leads to a distorted view of human behaviour.

For writers such as Burke (1969), Duncan (1968), Perinbanayagam (1974),

24

and Lyman and Scott (1975), however, the question is whether or not life is *like* theatre or life *is* theatre. For Lyman and Scott, at least the answer is clear:

'Dramatic performances typically carry their meanings by speech. So also the drama of human existence seems to require speech (communication in the broadest sense). And, by extension, the science of human affairs is largely a study of "performative utterances". Although they may be analytically separated, action and speech are inextricably intertwined in everyday affairs. In speech man manifests the clarification, motivation, exculpation and justification for action, and his own identity as well. Sociological analysis, thus, must treat the texts of ordinary performance. Social scientists who theorize within the framework of performance theory must behave, in the first instance, like an *audience* at a drama, they must pay special attention to the nature, order, meaning and consequences of gestures and speech and locate this scientific attitude in the attentiveness the philosophical spectator gives to the daily drama of human existence.

Some reality, then, is realized theatrically. Otherwise put, reality is a drama, life is theatre, and the social world is inherently dramatic.' (Lyman and Scott, 1975, pp. 2–3. Reproduced by permission of Oxford University Press.)

For Perinbanayagam (1974), too, the dramaturgical perspective implies much more than mere analogy. Following up the ideas of Burke (1966), he argues that words are utilized by social actors to persuade others and to induce their cooperation in sustaining a particular course of action. If this is taken to be a basic and characteristically human activity it should constitute the 'ontologistical basis of the human sciences'. Words, properties, settings, scenes, and behaviour are manipulated rhetorically, expressively, and dramatically to define a situation, establish a meaningful transaction and create an interaction. Thus, '. . . critics of the dramaturgical perspective err in supposing that the drama of social life is a mere metaphor (whatever that may be); it is rather the stuff and fibre of social relations, and the very substance of the sociological perspective invites consideration in dramatistic terms. . . .'

An Outline of My Argument

Based upon some of the ideas outlined above, in the rest of this book I shall seek to demonstrate the value of adopting a dramaturgical perspective on social life. I shall put forward and develop a model of the individual as 'performer' whose activities may be seen as so managed as to present a 'self' or 'character' to various audiences. My contention will be that, in the course of presenting his self to others, the individual social actor can be depicted as taking account of the 'scene', the 'setting', the 'props', and the 'cues' provided to him by other actors, and can be depicted as rehearsing and constructing his own performance in the light of his repertoire and of his ongoing interpretation of these various factors which, for him, constitute the situation.

I shall argue that *interaction*, the basis of social life, consists in the actor forging temporary working agreements with other actors as to the nature of the situation and the appropriateness of the various performances open to them. Such conscious activity I will term *strategic interaction*. More often than not, however, the appropriate performance occurs with little thought. It appears to be given in the form of a 'script'; there are, it would appear, scripts for almost any social contingency. Occasionally, however, the script is either missing or perceived to be deficient or unrewarding; hence the situation may be rendered problematic and the actors may strategically interact and mutually construct a revised performance. Such occasions are rare, but, I shall argue, particularly within organizations, many situations, even those normally thought to be closely scripted, are capable of being so revised.

The Dramaturgical Model of Man

Though of necessity my presentation has done violence to the subtleties of the various points of view crudely lumped together as being either systems based or humanistic, two clear and fundamentally disparate images of man persist. Man may be depicted as a passive neutral being subject to various forces and stimuli that impinge upon him and constrain his every action. Such an image is that of man as the helpless victim of Fate:

'This whole act's immutably decreed. 'Twas rehearsed by thee and me a billion years before the ocean rolled. Fool! I am Fate's lieutenant. I act under orders.' (Melville, 1948)

In direct contrast, man may be viewed as an active agent, a creative being selecting the stimuli to which he will respond, on earth not to fulfil Fate's dread command but to fulfil himself, to give birth and nurturance to his own potentialities and to achieve self-actualization.

The dramaturgical model of man is based upon the idea that man improvises his performance within the often very broad limits set by the scripts his society makes available to him. The dramaturgical analogy alerts us to the fact that the social actor is both character and agent; his part may be written for him but it cannot be realized without his agency. Once the actor performs, agency and character are fused and become one. The acquisition of the script is itself to be seen as a creative process in the sense that interpretation of events, relations, and situations are not predetermined in a fixed way for all time by any particular culture, although such interpretations may *appear* to be limited by conventional usage. Particular interpretations, however, are only sustained by continual affirmation and may be modified, changed, or transformed during the course of interaction.

The dramaturgical model of man is based upon a number of assumptions. The first is that interaction, face-to-face communication, is the foundation for the larger abstraction of social structure. In Schutz's (1962) terms:

'All the other manifold social relationships are derived from the originary experiencing of the totality of the other's self in the community of time and space. Any theoretical analysis of the notion of environment . . . would have to start from face-to-face relations as a basic structure of the world of daily life.'

Weinstein (1969) puts the point even more clearly and with equal assertiveness:

'If the sociologist's principal abstraction, social structure, has any concrete expression, it is to be found in myriad everyday social encounters. The operation of the larger system is dependent upon the successful functioning of the microscopic and episodic action systems generated in these encounters. And these in turn, require that participants are able to effectively pursue their personal goals. In the long view, if social structure is to be stable, individuals must be successful in achieving personal purposes.'

The dramaturgical perspective assumes that society can only be realized, that microscopic and episodic action can only occur, and that individual purposes can only be achieved through the sharing of meaning about particular events, situations, and relationships and that such sharing is realized symbolically, rhetorically, and dramatically. People in each other's presence take steps to ensure that others, party to the particular encounter or transaction, are made aware of their purposes and intentions, as they want them to be 'taken account of'. In any given interaction, social actors will take steps not only to present their own intentions and purpose but also to determine the identity and purposes of the other social actors involved. Each social actor makes the other aware and, in turn, is made aware of the other's identity and purposes by the taking of the necessary steps to publicize identities and intentions. Whatever the actor publicizes, either by dress, posture, gesture, or speech, becomes the data that the other actors, to revert to Weber's terminology, can 'take account of' and thereby can 'orient' their own behaviour accordingly:

'In other words the actor becomes aware of the other, as well as the other's subjective "experiences" *only to the extent that these experiences are dramaturgically available.* Interaction proceeds as the basis of *whatever it is that one takes to be the other's* subjective experience. . . .' (Perinbanayagam, 1974)

If the assumptions that society is composed of an infinite number of episodes or encounters and that in such face-to-face interactions purposes are expressed and defined dramaturgically are accepted, it seems to me that a number of consequences flow from them.

First, the most appropriate image of man is that which does justice to his expressive capacities, that of man the actor. To dramatize is to invite or proffer a particular identity, purpose, or definition of the situation to another who, in turn, dramatizes his intentions. As such, acting is not necessarily an attempt to manipulate others, nor to exploit them, though, of course, given this basic orientation man has the capacity to dissemble and to manage impressions. In most circumstances, however, the social actor is constrained to *be* what he offers as his identity, to *do* what he offers as his intentions, and to *mean* what he appears to define the situation as being. By the process of assimilation, often unconscious, he learns the situational scripts made available to him by the actors with whom he associates and acquires the ability to interpret and respond to the appropriate cues. In some circumstances he may seek to manipulate the scripts and the cues so as to achieve his own ends—he may adopt a strategic posture—but in many he acts spontaneously in accord with them or with personal scripts without question or detachment.

The dramaturgical model of man is primarily that of the person as a social actor seeking to bring into play *personal scripts* and/or responding to *situational scripts*. It contains the possibility exploited by analysts such as Goffman that man may also function as playwright, director, audience, and critic. As playwright, man fashions the scripts for the social stage and determines both what purposes he wishes to achieve and how best to achieve them. As director, each person seeks not only to cast his own role, endow his purposes with flesh and substance, but also to determine the way the parts for his fellow actors shall be performed by so managing the impression he makes as to constrain the responsive action of others. As audience the person can be aware of both his own and others' performances and, as critic, he can evaluate and comment (mentally or otherwise) upon them. The person is limited in the realization of his own purposes, however, by the fact that other persons may also be engaged in the encounter as playwrights, directors, audiences, and critics and may be competing with him for their own purposes. In such circumstances, for interaction to proceed at all, the person must take account of their expressions, their purposes, and intentions and seek to align his own activities with theirs, and, likewise, they with his (Lyman and Scott, 1975).

Thus, at the microscopic level of interaction and encounter, the reciprocal negotiation of meaning and identities embodies the notion of society being both determined and determiner. Meanings, identities, definitions, purposes, and intentions are, indeed, given, institutionalized, and shared, but are modified by negotiation and through interaction.

Such a view encompasses both the systems and the humanistic images of man. In many circumstances, perhaps even in most, the social actor is constrained by the scripts available to him, but in many, if not in most, he has the possibility of choice, the potential to create or revise his scripts. The dramaturgical image is not that of driven man, nor driving, isolated man, but of man as embedded in larger wholes—his family, his friends, his work groups, his community, and his country. This image of man contains the possibility of awareness of his condition implies that the individual actor may choose to conform or not to conform to the scripts offered to him by others, and in so doing may modify or transform them, a condition which, following Reisman (1953), I shall term 'autonomy'. The appropriate image of man is that he is neither the victim of fate nor, in some mystic fashion, self-actualized as the product of his own actions, but that he is a fashioner of drama, a symbolic communicator, a strutting player with the capacity to behave autonomously.

In putting forward the dramaturgical perspective I shall hope to demonstrate that it is a useful device or tool for the analysis of behaviour within organizations. I shall not be suggesting that what I am presenting is a model of the individual social actor's consciousness; my perspective is unlikely to be the perspective through which others in 'everyday situations' understand the world with which they are confronted. The utilization of the framework enables me to focus upon the creation and management of impressions as important features of social interaction, but it does not follow, nor am I seeking to imply, that the participants themselves necessarily utilize such a framework in either behaving or reflecting upon their behaviour.

Some social actors, confidence tricksters, spies, politicians, and salesmen may deliberately seek to exploit and manipulate impressions, but, for the most part, interaction proceeds smoothly on the basis that most of the parties to it are 'unconscious' or only dimly 'conscious' of their parts in creating, sustaining, and transforming impressions. Interaction, in many circumstances, has the quality of naturalness, a 'world-taken-for-granted' that would be the envy of many a stage actor seeking to present 'reality'.

I shall argue, however, that change occurs in circumstances where the natural, the world-taken-for-granted, is rendered problematic and is frightened out of its naturalness by alienation. Such circumstances can be created by encouraging social actors to utilize the dramaturgical framework and to adopt a *meta-theatrical* perspective whereby they can recognize the inherent theatricality of much of social life and see themselves as parties to social dramas—as creators of scripts, as directors, performers, audiences, and critics. In recognition and awareness lies the possibility of change: the possibility of creating new scripts, new directions, and new performances.

I am well aware that my choice of root metaphor, and the elaboration of it I am proposing in terms deriving from Goffman, leaves me open to the criticism outlined clearly by Biddle and Thomas (1966):

'The dramaturgical model, for instance, may easily go beyond the plausible implication that some behaviour is intentionally engaged in to foster given impressions and to achieve instrumental objectives, generally, to the extreme view that all human encounter is fraught with self-interest, calculation, manipulation, deception, guile, deceit and suspicion.'

To many what I have to say will suggest a sordid, disenchanted view of humans where society itself is reduced to nothing more than an act or a performance; in Macbeth's words:

'Life's but a walking shadow, a poor player
That struts and frets his hour upon the stage
And then is heard no more: it is a tale
Told by an idiot, full of sound and fury,
Signifying nothing.'

I believe that it is incontestable that each person has the capacity to manipulate, to cheat, and to observe cynically his own behaviour and that of others, and that in many cultures and subcultures such activities are indulged. It is equally incontestable that man has the capacity to plan, to speak the 'truth', and to adopt a caring attitude towards himself and others and that in many cultures and subcultures such activities are encouraged. Both views depend upon man's expressive abilities and both place man at the centre of events as a creative, adaptive being rather than as a puppet, automaton, or cog in the machine.

Summary

In this chapter I have briefly reviewed the utilization of the dramaturgical metaphor by a number of writers and have presented an outline of my ideas. I have been concerned to place man at the centre of the stage as both the *recipient* of scripts and the *agent*, as actor, of their realization.

Chapter **3**

Scripts, Whiffs, and Walnuts

I have argued earlier that familiarity breeds concepts; that the social scientist needs to develop an intimate relationship with his material if he is to derive concepts and understanding from it. Such familiarity is my starting point and in the following pages I will present some examples of recorded interaction from which I shall later seek to derive some concepts.

The first extract is from a regular top management meeting in a company which makes and sells drugs. We join them one afternoon as they are seated in the company boardroom discussing advertising budgets:

JOHN: (Head of the Trycyclin Division) *I'm not completely certain that we need as much as ninety thousand, in fact, to do the job. It could be that seventy, eighty thousand would probably do it. That . . .* (shows graph) *is a pattern showing what has happened to the sales of Trycyclin during the periods of advertising which are here and here, and you can see the effect that advertising has had, on the basis of one, two, three, four, five thousand of ex-stock sales; so that's a weekly rate of five thousand there, a weekly rate of three and three point two here. The advertising was put on here, it was put on here, and you can see the effect it has had. . . .*

ERIC: (Head of Diodin Division) (fidgets nervously, looks around at his colleagues, then interrupts) *I hate to be pedantic, John, but would we have sold, if we'd advertised the damn thing in January . . .* (laughs nervously) *. . . would we have sold some more in January . . .* (laughs) *. . . I mean what is the normal pattern of trading for stuff like that . . .* (laughs) *. . . I mean it is a bit also a seasonal effect which . . .* (continues to laugh) *. . . might. . . .*

(The rest of the group, with the exception of John, join in the laughter.)

JOHN: (coldly) *That is nothing to do with seasonal effect.*

ERIC: (stops laughing) *I mean, well, I can't see the dates on the bottom of your chart really. . . .*

JOHN: (pointing to parts of the chart) *That is March, that obviously is October to December, and quite clearly there would have been some growth, BUT Spring/Summer a year ago here and that is the same period again the year after advertising. . . .* (shows graph which indicates considerable rise)

ERIC: *Yes, well what I am saying is. . . .*

JOHN: *So you've got a base in a twelve-month period which shows that in that period, comparing like with like, you've got a base which has lifted four times. . . .*

FRANK: (Head of Vioticin) (with apparent innocence as though starting a new topic) *What do we estimate overall for Trycyclin for the winter would you say as a company. I mean each of us makes it and markets it geographically even though it's John's baby; what do we think we are going to move?*

ERIC: *Mine's a hundred and ten thousand units.*

JOHN: *Around two hundred thousand.*

FRANK: *For the season? Put me in, say, for a hundred. That's four hundred thousand packs . . .* (silence; then quietly, almost under his breath) *. . . for ninety thousand . . .*
(Silence. Frank doodles on his paper. Others regard the table.)

CHARLES: (the managing director and chairman of the meeting) *What point do you want to make?*

FRANK: *Well, nothing really . . . just seems it knocks a fair bit off the profit margin we are making by spending ninety thousand on four hundred thousand packs, that's all.*

JOHN: (somewhat angrily) *Look I don't know. . . .*

ERIC: (comes in quickly) *Look, I think you can split it another way. I mean there is an argument for saying that the company ought to split its advertising in another way and say that there is an essential thing and say that there is a thing such as brand leadership advertising. I think if you say that fifty thousand of that is brand leadership advertising, may be it is appropriate that it be split out into brand leadership advertising.*

FRANK: (conciliatory tone—John is huffing and puffing in the background) *Into prestige advertising.*

ERIC: *Into prestige advertising, yes. And OK we've got to look at it that way.*

MARTIN: (the finance director) *And you've got to put a product to it?*

ERIC: *Yes. . . .*

JOHN: (finding it difficult to contain himself) *Just to satisfy me. . . .*
(Laughter from all save John.)

JOHN: (continues through the noise) *. . . because I am concerned about the way this argument is going, how do we justify the rest of our advertising on a similar commercial basis?*
(Pause.)

FRANK: (toying with his pencil, recognizing the question is directed at him) *Well, we spend about one hundred and forty thousand pounds on a pill commercial and sell about four million packs. . . .*

JOHN: *And if you spend nothing on the commercial how many packs do you sell?*

FRANK: *In the fullness of time . . . none.*
(Silence.)

MARTIN: *What about your stuff John, do you have about thirty-five pence costed in . . . for advertising?*

JOHN: *What?*

MARTIN: *On Frank's figure just now, four hundred thousand for ninety thousand work out at about thirty-five pence per pack. . . .*

ANTHONY: (Market Research Manager) (dismissing the question with a wave of the hand) *Anyway as a company, we are short of things which lend themselves to good advertising. You know we are short of things that are good advertising. . . .*

FRANK: *Yes.*

ANTHONY: *I mean consumer credibility in the area of advertising has enormous pay-off in this area . . . we would really have to cut our budgets right down to see the effect at the end, and this would be one of the last. . . .*

ERIC: (seeking to interrupt the wandering tone of Anthony) *I, I. . . .*

ANTHONY: (cuts through) *In the short-term situation. . . .*

FRANK: (interrupts) *I think that there is a very good argument for saying for incremental extra sales you can afford to spend quite a lot of television advertising on this sort of activity, but I do think we must keep in our minds packs and pounds, that's all. I'm not saying I'm not for it, but I would like to think we've got a much better balance between pounds and packs in our minds.*
(Silence.)

MATHEW: (Administration Manager) *I think that's alright for, as it were, generating the cash, but I don't think it's alright for how you spend it. There are two issues here: obviously, one, you're getting it in from the public and that's your cash flow. Then the way in which you choose to spend it, can detach it. . . . I mean I don't wish to disagree with you* (looking at Frank who stares blankly at him) *but I think they are separate. . . .*

FRANK: *Oh yes. Very complicated. . . .*

MATHEW: *Very complicated. Yes. Comes to a judgement in the end. . . .*

JOHN: *The judgement comes all ways.* (addresses Frank loudly and with some considerable hostility) *Frank, look, I just do not see on the argument you have put forward this afternoon how you could POSSIBLY have put the advertising you put behind your Vioticin campaign. . . .*

FRANK: *I haven't argued anything this afternoon . . .* (laughs) *. . . I've just asked a few questions.*
(All laugh. Embarrassed silence.)

CHARLES: *"Well, let's move on. . . . On the organization issue. . . .*

I am not proposing to do anything with that material for the time being; I would like you to keep it in mind as you read the next extract which is comparatively brief.

The setting is a gatehouse to a large factory estate. I have stopped my car at the barrier, opened the door, climbed out, and am now approaching the glass screen behind which I can see the uniformed figure of a security guard. He speaks first:

GUARD: *Good morning sir.*
SELF: *Good morning.*
GUARD: *Quite a pleasant one as well now that the mist is clearing.*
SELF: *Yes, not too bad at all.*
GUARD: *Who is it you would like to see, sir?*
SELF: *Mr McDonald please.*
GUARD: *Which Mr McDonald, sir?*
SELF: *Pardon?*
GUARD: *Which Mr McDonald? We've two of them, sir.*
SELF: (slightly confused) *Oh, I didn't know. Mr McDonald in the Personnel Department.*
GUARD: *Oh yes, sir.* (He takes out a large book and begins to write in it.) *And you are . . .?*
SELF: *Mangham, M . . . A . . . N . . . G . . . H . . . A . . . M . . . .*
GUARD: *From?*
SELF: *The University of Bath. . . .*
GUARD: *University of Bath . . . to see . . .* (writes) *. . . Mr McDonald. . . .* (hands me an identification badge and an authorization chit) *I'll just ring through, sir, if you'll hang on a minute . . .* (dials) *. . . Oh, hello Mr McDonald, I have a Mr Mangham at the main gatehouse for you. . . .*

I trust that few of my readers will have difficulty in recognizing the last extract as an example of a routine piece of behaviour with which many of those who visit large companies will be familiar; it has the quality and predictability of a well-rehearsed drama.

A great deal of what passes for everyday interaction has this character, a feature which raises few if any questions about the meaning of the exchanges and presents little evidence of overt accommodation in the roles enacted. Much of everyday, taken-for-granted interaction proceeds on the basis of routines or *situational scripts* which may be defined as relatively predetermined and stereotyped sequences of action which are called into play by particular and well-recognized cues or circumstances, of which we acquire knowledge through the processes of socialization. I know my part in the gatehouse script and the guard knows his; I have learned what to expect of him and he of me or, to be more precise, of people like me. Even the unforeseen circumstance that there are two McDonalds creates little more than a ripple on the surface of the interaction. Both he and I have scripts for such contingencies.

In a similar fashion there is a classroom script, a railway station script, a talking-to-the-vicar-at-the-door-of-the-church script, there is a script for securing a job, one for purchasing a meal, and so on. Scripts are evolved to handle 'stylized everyday situations. Thus a script is a pre-determined, stereotyped sequence of actions that defines a well-known situation' (Schank and Abelson, 1977). They may be seen to occur where the situation is well specified, where more than one actor has to be accommodated, and where each of the actors understands what is supposed to happen. Each script has a minimum number of actors who are expected to assume and enact relatively clearly defined roles within the confines of the anticipated sequence of events. When certain sequences happen often enough, scripts come to be associated with the words or roles which create such sequences. Actors who do not have the familiarity with the situation cannot be expected to invoke the appropriate script, but can learn their parts (and those of others) by repeated involvements with the situations, or with circumstances taken to be somewhat familiar. There is an important human ability to transfer scripts from one setting to another. Football scripts can be apprehended by those with a familiarity with other games and worker/manager scripts may be generalized from one circumstance to another. We can be said to make sense of the world and reduce its equivocality by organizing the knowledge we have so as to fit each sequence of events into a situational script.

Few would doubt the script-like nature of the gatehouse interaction or of many of our everyday interactions; he or she who so doubts would benefit from reflecting for a moment on the actions they take upon waking, upon meeting others early in the morning at home, on the way to work, and at work. It will be a surprise if they do not discover that they are acting out a number of well-rehearsed parts in many situational scripts.

Many, however, may have difficulty in considering the first extract as an example of a situational script. What is routine and predictable about discussing the advertising budget? Without other extracts, without a close familiarity with the particular actors over time, it would, indeed, be unreasonable to make any inferences about the nature of the script being enacted by them. For the purpose of illustration let me provide a further short extract from the same group, this time discussing marketing plans.

ERIC: (Head of Diodin Division) *I . . . er . . . don't seem to have anything on that. . . .*

JOHN: *Nor do I.*

FRANK: *Nor me. . . .*

ANTHONY: (Market Research Manager) (muttering almost to himself) *No . . . I . . . er . . . haven't managed to get them out yet . . . pressure of work. The sales figures and. . . .*

CHARLES: (Managing Director) *When was the deadline for this . . . ?*

FRANK: (Head of Vioticin) *Eight or nine days ago wasn't it?*

JOHN: (Head of Trycyclin) (angrily) *certainly over a week ago.*

MARTIN: *I'll have it by next Wednesday or so.*

ERIC: (Head of Diodin) (laughing)
A good couple of weeks after we said we needed it. . . . Still better late. . . .
*(*Laughter. Silence.)

CHARLES: *OK. Let's move on to looking at. . . .*

Repeated associations with this group may lead one to infer that their interactions do have a pattern, that their meetings do have a situational script. One aspect of that script, for example, may relate to how they handle conflict in the group. It may be that it is always accompanied by the kind of approach and withdrawal manifested in both of the extracts—aggression followed by laughter and silence. It could be that their meetings regularly fail to resolve issues, that the remarks of the Market Research Manager are ignored almost as a matter of routine, that the raising of potentially controversial issues is always accompanied by someone seeking to head off open conflict, and so on. The nature of the script enacted by these particular actors may be more complex and convoluted than that enacted between myself and the gatekeeper, but careful observation of this interaction may reveal that it is just as patterned, predetermined, and predictable.

The extracts may also be used to illustrate examples of both *personal scripts* and *strategic scripts*. The former concept is, like situational scripts, derived from the work of Schank and Abelson (1977). Personal scripts consist of performances which lead to satisfaction on the part of the main actor; the actor may not be conscious of his personal script, but it is nearly always something he has sought to act out repeatedly. If it is not too much of a contradiction it can be claimed that there are some common personal scripts. The words and actions which accompany the performance of the flatterer (or creep), the smooth-talking romancer, the jealous spouse, the poor downtrodden female, and so on, are examples of the stock of personal scripts. In a restaurant script, for example, a particular actor's personal script may lead him to flirt with the waitresses. Some personal scripts are less common, but still recognizable. Eric, for instance, in the extract quoted about characteristically displays a nervousness and plays out in many circumstances the part of the diffident. John, on the other hand, may be seen to be following a sort of angry-young-man personal script. Repeated observation of these performances over a range of situations may enable the observer to conclude that these are indeed not atypical actions but the acting out of personal scripts.

Clearly the personal script may be very personal indeed and, as such, if performed compulsively, may become the focus of attention for the clinical psychologist. For my purposes I am interested in the personal script insofar as it enters into situational scripts. The personal script of Charles, the Managing Director, appears to consist of doing very little and saying nothing and such a performance over time cannot fail to have an effect upon the situational script of the management meeting.

Frank's performance provides the opportunity for the introduction of a third category, that of the strategic script. His apparently innocent question, 'What do we estimate overall . . .?', may be designed to bring about certain other pieces of behaviour on the part of his colleagues. Such performances differ from personal scripts in that the actor is conscious of what he is doing and what he is trying to achieve through his actions. The performance has an element of planning and even of manipulation that is not found in either situational scripts or personal scripts.

Of course, there can be circumstances where the actor in pursuit of a personal script within a situational script utilizes a strategic script. For example, the predatory male or female may wish to convert the gatehouse script into a setting for the utilization of his or her flirtation scripts. To so do may require that he or she actually consciously plans to create the conditions where such a script can more easily be brought into play.

Personal scripts and strategic scripts share a common interest in restricting the potential range of performance of other social actors in the situation. Eric's personal script, marked as it is by diffidence and a desire to avoid open conflict, makes it difficult for anyone else to respond with open aggression. It has a quality of 'please don't hit me' which effectively blocks any such response. In a similar fashion the social actor may seek to cast others into particular responses: the combative approach of John, the almost continuous presentation of an angry-young-man personal script, may be seen as an attempt (quite unconscious, of course, but learned over the years) to constrict and constrain the responses of others into areas which he feels able to perform effectively. He or she who is always performing a personal script of asking for help often succeeds in pulling help from others; he who frequently plays the fool more often than not constrains others to respond by laughing; and so on.

Strategic scripts are more *consciously* concerned with influencing the response of others. The salesman or the politician may quite deliberately plan and rehearse his performance in order to achieve certain ends. Frank, in the extract quoted above, may be indulging in a little strategic interaction (John's response and, to a lesser extent, that of Charles indicate that they consider his behaviour to be leading somewhere). Put somewhat crudely, he can be seen to be manipulating the situation for his own ends; asking apparently innocent questions is an effective ploy. Frank's behaviour *may* be seen (without access to his views we cannot be more dogmatic) as an attack upon John's advertising expenditure. The situational script forbids direct confrontation, so Frank indulges in an oblique approach. He succeeds in baiting John and really brings the situation back to manageable proportions by deflating him when he responds with direct aggression:

'I haven't argued anything this afternoon . . . (laughs) . . .
I've just asked a few questions.'

Scripts are acquired through the process of assimilation and formal learning. Events may be said to make sense and to have meaning when the actors can call upon the appropriate script or scripts. Most routine scripts are well known to the actors who are required to participate, and most have associated with them subroutines or satellite scripts which are brought into play should an obstacle or error occur in the main drama. Schank and Abelson (1977) term these departures from the main script *what-ifs* or *whiffs*. For example the normal situational script for the management meeting may be for them to steer away from conflict; but what if John persists in attacking Frank and refuses to be deflected by the laughter? No doubt another script along the lines of 'Look let's not get heated about this' or 'Perhaps you and I ought to discuss this out of this meeting' would be evoked and followed.

The following extract from *The Fall and Rise of Reginald Perrin* (Nobbs, 1976) illustrates very well the lengths the human actor will go to in order to fit even the most unusual 'whiffs' into a recognisable script:

'Joan ushered Mr Campbell-Lewiston in. He was wearing a lightweight grey suit and carried a fawn German raincoat. When he smiled Reggie noticed that his teeth were yellow.

"How are things going in Germany?" said Reggie.

"It's tough," said Mr Campbell-Lewiston. "Jerry's very conservative. He doesn't go in for convenience foods as much as we do."

"Good for him."

"Yes, I suppose so, but I mean it makes our job more difficult."

"More of a challenge," said Reggie.

Joan entered with a pot of coffee on a tray. There were three biscuits each—a bourbon, a rich tea and a custard cream.

"There are some isolated regional breakthroughs,"said Mr Campbell-Lewiston.

"Some of the mousses are holding their own in the Rhenish Palatinate, and the flans are cleaning up in Schleswig-Holstein."

"Oh good, that's very comforting to know," said Reggie.

"And what about the powdered Bakewell Tart mix, is it going like hot cakes?"

"Not too well, I'm afraid."

Reggie poured out two cups of coffee and handed one to his visitor. Mr Campbell-Lewiston took four lumps of sugar.

"And how about the tinned treacle pudding—is that proving sticky?"

"Oh very good. Treacle tart sticky. You're a bit of a wag," said Mr Campbell-Lewiston, and he laughed yellowly.

Suddenly the penny dropped.

"Good God," said Reggie. "Campbell-Lewiston. I thought the name was familiar. Campbell-Lewiston, E. L. Ruttingstagg. The small bore rifle team."

"Of course. Goofy Per . . . R. I. Perrin."

They shook hands.

"You're doing pretty well for yourself," said Reggie.

"You too," said E. L. Campbell-Lewiston.

"You were a nauseous little squirt in those days," said Reggie.

E. L. Campbell-Lewiston drew in his breath sharply.

"Thank heaven for small bores, for small bores grow bigger every day," said Reggie. "What?"

"I really must congratulate you on the work you're doing in Germany," said Reggie.

"Do you remember the time you bit me in the changing room?"

"I don't remember that."

"I think you've done amazingly well with those flans in Schleswig-Holstein," said Reggie. "And now what I'd like you to do is pave the way for our new range of exotic ices. There are three flavours—mango delight, cumquat surprise and strawberry and lychee ripple."

"I can't believe it. I've never bitten anyone."

Reggie stood up and spoke dynamically.

"Aren't you listening?" he said. "I'm talking about our new range; of ice creams."

"Oh, yes. Sorry," said E. L. Campbell-Lewiston.

"I'd like you to try it out in a typical German town," said Reggie. "Are there any typical German towns??"

"All German towns are typical," said E. L. Campbell-Lewiston.

Reggie sipped his coffee thoughtfully, and said nothing. E. L. Campbell-Lewiston waited uneasily.

"Is there any particular way you want me to handle the new ice creams?" he asked at length.

"Wanking much these days, are you?" asked Reggie.

"I beg your pardon?"

"We used to call you the phantom wanker. No wonder you could never hit the bloody target."

E. L. Campbell-Lewiston stood up. His face was flushed.

"I didn't come here to be insulted like that," he said.

"Sorry," said Reggie. "I'll insult you like this, then. You don't clean your teeth properly, you slovenly sod."

"Just who do you think you are?" said E. L. Campbell-Lewiston.

"I think I'm the man in charge of the new exotic ices project," said Reggie. "I'm the man who's expecting you to take Germany by storm, and I have every confidence you will. I was tremendously impressed by your article on the strengths and limitations of market research in the International Deep Freeze News."

"Oh thank you."

They stood up and Reggie handed Mr Campbell-Lewiston his raincoat.

"Yes, I found your analysis of the chance element inherent in any random sample very persuasive."

"I hoped it was all right."

At the door E. L. Campbell-Lewiston turned and offered Reggie his hand.

"Er . . . all this . . . I mean, is it some kind of new middle management technique?" he asked.

"That's right," said Reggie. "It's the new thing. Try it out on the Germans." '

(Reproduced by persmission of Victor Gollanz Ltd.)

The illustration may be a little difficult to accept. If so the work of McHugh (1958) on defining the situation may cause you to revise any hasty dismissal you may feel prone to. McHugh revealed, by means of an ingenious series of experiments, just what lengths people will go to in order to make sense of encounters, in order, that is, to fit apparently unusual *whiffs* into more understandable scripts. His subjects were involved in psychotherapy interviews where they were constrained to form questions to the psychotherapist (in another room) capable of being answered 'yes' or 'no'. After each response the subjects were invited to speculate upon the implications of the response. What they were not aware of was the random nature of the psychotherapist's responses. Many of the subjects expended great effort in seeking to place these responses within an intelligible framework. Without doubt poor old Campbell-Lewiston has many peers in the laboratory and in the hurly-burly of everyday social interaction. There are, it would seem, scripts for very many of the ordinary 'whiffs' and even scripts for some of the most extraordinary.

Thus there is not widespread failure to fit lines of action to each other because we each strive to accommodate the behaviour of the other, because we each assume the behaviour of the other to have some meaning if only we can fit it into the appropriate script. Blumer (1969) has outlined how different individual acts come to fit together:

'Their alignment does not occur through sheer mechanical juggling, as in the shaking of walnuts in a jar or through unwitting adaptation. Instead, the participants fit their acts together, first, by identifying the social act in which they are about to engage, and second, by interpreting each other's acts in forming the joint act. By identifying the social act or joint action the participant is able to orient himself....' (Herbert Blumer, *Symbolic Interactionism: Perspective and Method*, © 1969. By permission of Prentice-Hall, Inc., Englewood Cliffs, New Jersey.)

Once identified the interaction can proceed and the social actor is on familiar territory and can play his part without anxiety.

'Estragon: So long as one knows.
Vladimir: One can bide one's time.
Estragon: One knows what to expect.
Vladimir: No further need to worry.'

(Beckett, 1956)

Summary

In this chapter I have presented some examples of interaction and have sought to indicate briefly the kind of concepts I shall be dealing with in the rest of the book. I have introduced the terms *situational script, personal script, strategic script,* and *whiffs* and have hinted at some of the dynamics of interaction. In the next chapter I will explore some of these in considerably more detail.

Chapter 4

Interaction as Drama

In the previous chapter I suggested that much of that which passes for everyday social intercourse may be conceptualized in terms of the performance of situational and personal scripts. I further suggested that such interaction often proceeded smoothly, 'naturally' and without the social actors involved within such performances necessarily or even usually being aware of the script-like bases of their interactions. I raised the idea of strategic scripts as a way of accommodating the abnormal circumstances where one or more actors are aware of the nature of their performances and are seeking to exploit the dynamics of such performances to mutual or individual advantage.

In this chapter I wish to propose a form of ideal-typical model of the process of interaction based upon the abnormal or atypical, the form of interaction I have termed *strategic*. What follows therefore is a model of conscious and deliberate behaviour, behaviour as it might be if all performances were carefully constructed, carefully maintained, and consciously changed. I am arguing, in effect, that behaviour may be carefully planned and rehearsed and may be highly conscious and deliberate—may, in fact, be strategic and manipulative; the extent that it is is a matter for empirical investigation.

Basically I intend to argue that interaction proceeds somewhat like the unfolding of a stage drama, by a process of 'contingent response' whereby what A says or does provokes a response in B to which A, in turn, responds, and so on. There is a danger in putting the issue quite as baldly as that since it implies a linear development which is not always necessarily the case. In presenting his behaviour the first actor may be taking into account the possible reactions of the second actor and, because of this, it is impossible to say what is cause and effect. Dipping into the stream of interaction and seeking to examine a particular element disturbs the nature of the process: what is stimulus, what is response, what is sent, what is received, what is cause, what is effect, is dependent upon a temporary and arbitrary freezing of the system. Interaction is a process, not a structure, and may be conceived of as a seamless web, each participant affected by and simultaneously affecting each other participant. Though convenient and, indeed, given the linear nature of language, the only form available to us, an analysis which sees interaction proceeding by 'your turn, my turn, his turn' exchange is inaccurate and does less than justice to the process. 'All persons are engaged in sending (encoding) and receiving (decoding) messages *simultaneously*.

Each person is constantly sharing in the encoding and decoding process, and each person is affecting the other' (Wenburg and Wilmot, 1973). The process is one of simultaneous transaction.

What the social actor does in a given encounter, therefore, is a product of the cues he perceives—what he interprets to be the purpose of the behaviour of other actors and the meanings the scene conveys to him (the situational script)—and the roles he has in his repertoire and is disposed to play (his personal script). With the qualifications introduced above, *for the purposes of analysis*, interaction could be said to proceed by a cycle of cues and interpretation or definition of these cues on the part of the various social actors in the situation.

In effect I am arguing that an adequate description of face-to-face interaction must take into account both the situational and the personal script. Performances are shaped by both of these elements, but may be changed, as I shall argue later, by the actor adopting a strategic stance in relation to these scripts. Scripts are the results of attempts at coordination of actions occurring between actors; strategic interaction both creates and transforms them.

A Simple Model of Social Interaction

The starting point is the model of dyadic social interaction illustrated in Figure 1. Analytically, one may begin at any point within the cycle, but for the sake of clarity of exposition I propose to begin at the top and work clockwise back to this position.

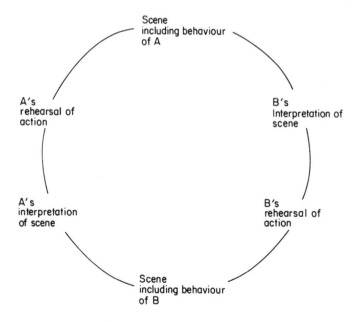

Figure 1

The Characteristics of the Individual Social Actor

An important part of the scene consists of A's behaviour. A does something and strings together a set of behaviours which, theoretically, at least, can be inferred to be the expression of some desirable goal on the part of A. (In part, what A does, of course, is a consequence of *his* interpretation of the scene, but for the purpose of analysis and explanation a beginning must be made which does not immediately lead back to the prior state.) By controlling his expressive behaviour, social actor A seeks to project an image of the role he desires to assume in the scene. Following Goffman (1959) we can call this process the selective *presentation of self*. In effect A's presentation says, 'This is who I wish to be taken for in this interaction.' It also says, 'And this is who I take you to be', for not only does A's behaviour express an image of what A wishes to be taken for but in so doing it implies a complementary role for B. In effect, the part A wishes to play can be seen to be based upon his ideas about the part that B ought to play, and his action may be seen as conceived and executed so as to direct or cast B into behaving appropriately. Following Weinstein and Deutschberger (1964) we can term such a process *altercasting*.

The behaviour that A brings into play, the role which he wishes to assume, and that which he allocates to B will be the product of both his repertoire and the opportunities he perceives to employ it. Put somewhat simply, what happens depends upon what each actor brings to the scene, his personal scripts, and what opportunities present themselves or can be created. In theatrical terminology it can be said that the actors may be type-cast for particular parts. Their repertoire of scripts and gestures may be limited and the range of parts they can take on may be restricted: some may be limited to being heroes, some to villains, and some to fools.

The range of parts available to the particular actor, his personal scripts or repertoire, is constrained by and is ultimately related to his view of himself being and acting in that particular scene. In less fuzzy terms, his repertoire is related to his self-concept.

The Self as Director

The idea of the *self* is of central if disputed importance in sociology and social psychology and, not surprisingly, has therefore been defined severally. My own concern is with what has been called the 'social self'. The basic premise is that the self-concept is social in origin. In Berger's (1963) terms: 'identity is socially bestowed, socially sustained and socially transformed'. The self-concept evolves in response to the evaluations others make concerning our behaviour. According to Mead (1956) each and every person comes to know himself only through the responses of others. Our repertoire is governed by the audiences with whom we interact. Naturally we do not value the reactions of all people equally; we pay more attention to the opinions and attitudes of important people in our lives, 'significant others', than to opinions in general. Nonetheless, the 'generalized other' does affect self-definition. Both are important sources of self-definition. According to Mead (1956):

'. . . there are two general stages in the full development of the self. At the first of these stages, the individual's self is constituted simply by an organization of the particular attitudes of other individuals toward himself and toward one another in the specific social acts in which he participates with them. But at the second stage in the full development of the individual's self that self is constituted not only by an organization of these particular individual attitudes, but also by an organization of the social attitudes of the generalized other or the social group as a whole to which he belongs.'

Cooley (1964) reinforces the notion that the self-concept is social in origin and persistence with his widely discussed notion of the 'looking-glass self'. He suggests that the attitudes and reactions of others are important to the individual's self-concept in a 'reflective' manner. The attitudes, feelings, and evaluations of others are reflected as though we were looking into a mirror and evaluating ourselves. Significant others constitute the 'mirror' from which we obtain the reflection and, by inference, the evaluation. We try to see the impact of our behaviour on others and to *impute* a sentiment towards which we in turn react emotionally. 'The thing that moves us to pride or shame is not the mere mechanical reflection of ourselves, but an *imputed* sentiment the imagined effect of this reflection upon another's mind' (Cooley, 1964).

The assertion is that while man's biologic characteristics may provide certain conditions which are necessary to the formation of self-awareness (e.g. a complex brain), man must be exposed to social life in order to acquire a self-concept. Humans learn to be human through association with each other; humans acquire ways of defining self through socialization. The self-concept is the more or less organized set of descriptions and concepts an individual has of and for himself.

I say more or less organized because other actors have provided us with a number of scripts and a range of possible roles. An individual may have some sense of personal integrity and continuity, but will typically use a large number of different concepts to describe himself and his behaviour. His descriptions will be influenced by what he takes to be the nature of his audience:

'This is evident from the fact that the character and weight of that other, in which mind we see ourselves, makes all the difference with our feelings. We are ashamed to seem evasive in the presence of a straightforward man, cowardly in the presence of a brave one, gross in the eyes of a refined one, and so on.' (Cooley, 1964)

It follows that behaviour may vary from scene to scene; indeed, it is more likely to show variability than not, since the individual actor learns specific and idiosyncratic scripts:

'The learning approach holds that a person can acquire varying conceptions of self in different situations. He can learn a certain way of conceptualizing himself from his father and possibly an opposite way from his younger brothers. In the former case he may come to see himself as "submissive" and in the latter "dominant".' (Gergen, 1971)

The definitions that an individual has for himself develop from specific situational concepts. For example, the definition an actor has of himself relative to his ability to direct and lead others develops in situations in which he has sought to act out direction and leadership. If an actor performs poorly in a number of such situations his desire to undertake such a script in the future is (other things being equal) likely to diminish. In effect his less than adequate performance results in negative or critical audience response, and his negative evaluation is incorporated into the self-definition. Accordingly, the actor who holds a negative self-definition of his capacity to direct and lead will choose to avoid circumstances which call for this part to be played by him or will choose to reinterpret such scenes in line with scripts he feels more positive about offering. Thus the self-concept becomes directive:

'One thing that distinguishes man from the lower animals is the fact that he has a conception of himself, and once he has defined his role he strives to live up to it. He not only acts, but he dresses the part, assumes quite spontaneously all the manners and attitudes that he convenes as proper to it. . . .' (Park, 1927)

Providing that there is related consistency in the attitudes of others towards the actor the self will not be in flux. As Rogers (1961) puts it:

'As long as the self-gestalt is firmly organized, and no contradictory material is even dimly perceived, then positive self-feelings may exist, the self may be seen as worthy and acceptable, and conscious tension is minimal. Behaviour is consistent with the organized hypotheses and concepts of the self-structure.'

Self-defence and Role-behaviour

Given a 'firmly organized' self-concept, I am suggesting that what each actor brings to an encounter is, at the very least, a desire to maintain the integrity of that self-concept by bringing into play those scripts which he values.

The individual actor seeks support for the claims that he makes for his self-concept. The scripts each actor seeks to bring into play in any particular encounter, therefore, are those which support his view of how he sees himself behaving and feeling in that kind of encounter.

Modes of engaging with others are learned in infancy and childhood. The individual acquires certain behaviours and practices, and becomes accomplished at certain roles and actively seeks opportunities to bring them into play. As Beier (1966) confirms: 'An individual's preferred modes of interaction are not merely defenses; they are also behaviours that seek out certain responses in the environment.' In order to reduce uncertainty, the actor may behave so as to cast others in a very narrow range of response. His predispositions consist in large part of a series of preferred modes of engagement which have been evolved to trigger responses which he can handle.

It is difficult to state unequivocally when the individual repertoire is complete—when, that is, the directing aspect of the self has acquired a relatively stable set of self-definitions. For some the process goes on well into adult life; for most it is probably complete relatively early in adulthood. Once established, once the valued scripts have been refined and accepted as an integral part of the social actor, they tend to be not only directive but also relatively resistant to change. I am not suggesting that particular new scripts may not be learned or that old ones may not be revalued, adapted or modified; clearly this does happen. Rather I am saying that radical reorientation, major departures from the scripts which involve a major shift in the individual's perception of who he is and what he is capable of, are unlikely to occur.

Behaviour may thus become, in one form or another, conscious or unconscious, an attempt to constrain and constrict 'Alter'—the other—and to reduce Alter's discretion to respond through influencing, often covertly and subtly, *his* interpretation of the scene. Since a large part of the scene for B is A's behaviour it is in A's interest to so manage his presentation as to protect himself in the unfolding interaction—to seek, that is, by controlling his own behaviour, to direct the behaviour of the other actor along lines that he considers appropriate. Goffman (1959) is worth repeating in this context:

'Regardless of the particular objective which the individual has in mind . . . it will be in his interests to control the conduct of others, especially their responsive treatment of him. This control is achieved largely by influencing the definition of the situation which others come to formulate, and he can influence this definition by expressing himself in such a way as to give them the kind of impression that will lead them to act voluntarily in accordance with his own plan.'

So we have a circumstance whereby each social actor party to a particular interaction arrives equipped to play certain parts in relation to himself and to evaluate these performances on the basis of his previous idiosyncratic experience. Not only is each actor *equipped* to play certain parts but he is *predisposed* to a certain repertoire. With this in mind we can turn now to the characteristics of the scene and the interpretative process.

The Characteristics of the Scene

In a sense, the interpretation of the scene is a 'given' not a process. Social actors know how to behave; they have their parts handed down to them for this or that scene from generation to generation. As Blumer (1969) has it, there is not widespread 'failure to fit lines of action' to each other since many, if not most, of the situations encountered by individuals are 'given': that is to say, the process of socialization teaches the appropriate scripts to be invoked when faced by situations A, B, and C. Many situations have been faced by the group or the society living together over generations, and many actors have scripted the possible definitions or interpretations. From this experience has arisen a consensus about what is and what is not appropriate performance in particular, common scenes. Schutz (1967) refers to this aspect of social life as the 'reciprocity of perspectives' by which he refers to 'What is supposed to be known in common by everyone who shares our system of relevances . . . the way of life considered to be the natural, the good, the right one by the members of the "in group".' Thomas (1923) considers the 'situation' as straightforward and easy to understand:

'Preliminary to any self-determined act of behaviour there is always a stage of examination and deliberation which we may call "the definition of the situation". And actually not only concrete acts are dependent upon the situation, but gradually a whole life-policy and the personality of the individual himself follow from a series of such definitions. . . .
The family is the smallest social unit and the primary defining agency. As soon as the child has free action and begins to pull, tear, muddle, and prowl, the parents begin to define the situation through speech and other signs and pressures: "Be quiet", "Sit up straight", "Blow your nose", 'Answer your mother", "Be kind to your sister", etc. This is the real significance of Wordsworth's phrase "Shades of the prison house begin to close upon the growing child." His wishes and activities begin to be inhibited, and gradually, by definitions within the family, by playmates, in the school, in the Sunday School, in the community, through reading, by formal instruction, by informal signs of approval and disapproval, the growing member learns the code of his society.'

Berne (1964) and other writers have noted the strength and stability of patterns of interaction and have characterized them as 'scripts' or 'games'. The participants engage each other and behave towards each other as though there were no other possible behaviours open to them.

Such codes and scripts are the world-taken-for-granted: they constitute the common sense of particular groups and societies in particular locations and particular historical epochs. Such situational scripts are deeply embedded in the linguistic systems utilized by social actors. Indeed, linguistic systems do little more than codify the categories of analysis, the ways of thinking, and the consensual definitions arrived at by these various groupings. As a result language itself does not merely reflect scripts; it shapes them. This must be so to the extent that language systems grow out of the collective life of a specific group as they interact; scripts arise from group life and return as folkways, mores taboos, collective representations, group attitudes, laws, etc., to influence the elaboration of other scripts.

To *influence* rather than to *determine* since Thomas' formulation and the discussion of the impact of linguistic systems leads directly to tautologies of the following form: interpretations arise from the culture, become part of it, and therefore cause other interpretations. Such a view is far too deterministic. The *process* of interpretation is, of course, interpenetrated by preexisting interpretations, often encapsulated in the language of the particular group or society, but the process insofar as it is an interactive one—a dynamic, negotiated process—allows for the modification or revision of interpretations. The social actor, whether child or adult, does not learn his parts and does not assimilate his scripts in isolated scenes or situations but as a person in a continuous state of experiencing. It follows that no one can experience the 'same' thing as someone else; nor can any one person experience 'the same situation' twice. Actors are not alike and actors mature in terms of experience; having experienced 'the same situation' before they can no longer view it as they viewed it the first time around. Each actor is at any one time the culmination of what Schutz (1967) terms his 'biographic process', which is the 'life history as actually lived and experienced in the succession of his innumerable successive involvements with many kinds of situations and people within many areas of life activities' (Wagner, 1973).

Interpretations are learned within specific contexts and meanings arise from the responses of particular audiences. However *common* the interpretation, however taken for granted the meaning, it is always and inevitably influenced by the fine gauze of individual experience. The individual actor learns the 'meaning' of, say, participation at point X in his biographic process in circumstances A, in association with actor P. It is logically and empirically impossible for any other actor to have the same experience. Since other actors are, in turn, products of *their* biographic processes it is, to say the least, unlikely that there will be complete agreement as to the interpretations of particular scenes. This will be even less likely if it is accepted that the 'biographic process' implies that each of us is subject to subtle but real change in our interpreting processes as a result of experiences.

Perception and interpretation are, beyond all else, selective processes:

'Actors create and constitute the environment to which they react: the environment is put there by the actors within the organization and by no one else. This reasserts the argument that the environment is a phenomenon tied to processes of attention, and that, unless something is attended to, it doesn't exist.' (Weick, 1969)

Even those with relatively little differentiation of scripts rarely utilize them all the time. A way of seeing the world, a particular schema, may vary in its salience to the individual at any given moment. Salience is affected by familiarity and previous successful utilization of the concept, by the context, and by motivation. If my past experience has convinced me that a particular way of seeing events is functional, I will tend to repeat this. Since scripts are learned in specific situations, similar contexts will tend to stimulate the use of the learned concepts. The third influence is motivation; if, in financial need, situations may be conceptualized in terms of their economic return, if hungry or in need of friendship, other concepts may be utilized.

The interpretation of the scene at which any individual arrives is a product of the total range of scripts available to him and the salience of a number of them. To the extent that different individuals have different experiences and, thus, different scripts available to them we would not expect one-to-one correspondence with regard to the interpretation of a scene, though it should not be forgotten that many scenes are strongly defined culturally and leave little apparent room for individual interpretation.

In my terms, the social stage may be said to consist of settings, costumes, and properties which guide the social actors to arriving at the appropriate script to bring into play.

The setting, for example, as Steele (1973) points out, is a cue to the type of interaction expected there. The architectural design, the furniture, the decor all contribute to the cueing of the appropriate script. For example, the physical characteristics of the reading room of the British Museum are not conducive to the enactment of frivolity; high seriousness of settings thus contribute to the evocation of seriousness of script.

The importance of costumes as script definers is also well attested in social life. The wearing of a boiler suit to a formal dinner is a comment upon formal dinner scripts. Uniforms of all kinds, military or otherwise, function so as to cue appropriate responses, as does make-up, hairstyle, and personal adornment (or, in some circumstances, lack of it).

Properties such as stethoscopes, micrometers, briefcases, swagger sticks, and so on, equally serve as devices to define roles and cue the selection of particular scripts. It is important to remember, however, that cues of whatever form serve only as a guide or aid to the social actor's selection of a particular script. They do not determine it any more than A's behaviour determines B's response. Scenes are interpreted, not simply recorded.

The Imputation of Role to Self and Others

The interpretation an individual places upon events is a working hypothesis, a preliminary to his own action which, in effect, puts his hypothesis to the test of experience. The social actor, in arriving at his working hypothesis, may seek the answer to a number of questions (Stebbins, 1969):

(1) Who is present? In the sense of not only who is physically present but who is part of the interaction?

(2) What do these relevant Alters construe the situation to be?

(3) What are the intentions of the relevant Alters? What do they appear to want from the interaction?

(4) What are the strategies and tactics likely to be employed by the Alters to achieve their ends?

(5) What appear to be Alters' justification for their actions?

(6) In the light of the foregoing what do I, Ego, take the situation to be?

(7) What do I wish to achieve?

(8) How am I going about achieving desired outcomes, i.e. what are my plans?

(9) How can I justify them?

(10) How am I, Ego, seen by Alter?

(11) What evaluation of the situation is imputed to me by Alter? That is, I may evaluate the situation as being of type X, but I also seek to know whether or not Alter perceives me as evaluating it as type X or some other type N.

(12) Similarly, I am interested in Alter's perception of my intentions and

(13) Alter's perception of my plans and actions and
(14) Alter's perception of my justification.

There is a reciprocity about all of this which is well caught by Westlake's (1966) statement: 'I know this, and he knows that I know it, and I know that he knows I know it, and so on through an infinity of facing mirrors, each of us aware of the receding levels of the other's knowledge. . . .'
Put somewhat shortly, Ego seeks to know what Alter takes a particular situation to be, in order to predict and understand what Alter's response to any course of action elaborated by Ego may be. Briefly, Laing (1969) captures the complexity of the process of interpretation:

'Even an account of one person cannot afford to forget that each person is always calling upon others and acted upon by others. . . . The person whom we describe, and over whom we theorize, is not the only agent in his "world". How he perceives and acts toward the others, how they perceive and act toward him, how he perceives them as perceiving him, how they perceive him as perceiving them, are all aspects of the "situation". They are all pertinent to understanding one person's participation in it.'

As Stebbins (1969) notes, all of these perceptions by a given set of actors can, *theoretically*, be part of their interpretations of a particular scene, but are not necessarily obtainable by any actor or set of actors. Ego might be unable to divine the intentions of Alter and may not be able to apprehend the justification for his tactics within a given situation, so he will necessarily have to operate on limited data in making his own interpretation. He will, nonetheless, continue to scan the situation and construct a series of differential diagnoses as the encounter develops in an attempt to improve his interpretations and enhance his predictions.
Let us return to our basic encounter and consider a simplified interpretative process from the point of view of B. A, it will be recalled, has assumed a role for himself and his role performance carries with it a projection of what he takes B to be. To determine the opportunities for himself in this situation B seeks to understand what A is projecting and what implications that role has for B. The stage actor does something similar when he attempts to build up his role:

'When the actor examines the text to prepare his part, he looks for what makes the words different from conversation; that is, he looks for the structural elements of the building, for links of characteristics thought in the character and so on. He persists till he has shaped in his mind a firm and workable pattern of his part.' (Styan, 1963)

Stanislavsky (1950) called these clues to interpretation, the 'subtext' of the play: 'The "subtext" is a web of innumerable, varied inner patterns inside a play . . . it is the subtext that makes us say the words we do in a play.'
B is doing something of the same sort when he interacts with A. He is seeking to interpret A's role and the role-performance implications for himself. Turner (1962), in the symbolic interactionist tradition, calls the process 'role-taking':

'Behaviour is said to make sense when a series of actions is interpretable as indicating that the actor has in mind some role which guides his behaviour. . . . The isolated actions becomes a datum for role-analysis only when it is interpreted as the manifestation of a configuration. . . . The unifying element is to be found in some assignment of purpose or sentiment to the actor. . . . Role-taking involves selective perception of the action of another and a great deal of selective emphasis, organized about some purposes or sentiment attributed to the other.'

To interpret effectively B seeks to be able to take A's role and he seeks to understand thoroughly A's intention and action in order to understand its implications for himself, just as A must understand B's position. Such mutual role taking is the prerequisite for effective communication and interaction.

B, like the stage actor, is looking for the structural elements and is seeking to group the subtextual stream of images and ideas that will enable him to define who A is and what role A assumes to be acceptable at this stage of the encounter. He does this by paying attention not only to the content of what A says, but also by listening to the tone of his voice, seeking to pick up emotional overtones and affective clues, and by paying attention to other covert and extra forms of communication.

It is important to distinguish, as B no doubt does, between A's intended performance, the information he consciously and deliberately 'gives' and the information he 'gives off';

'The first involves verbal symbols or their substitutes which he uses admittedly and solely to convey the information. . . . The second involves a wide range of action that others can treat as symptomatic of the actor, the expectation being that the action was performed for reasons other than the information conveyed in this way.' (Goffman, 1959)

A may seek to give the message that he wishes to lead and dominate, but the impression he 'gives off', paralinguistically, posturally or proximally, may fail to reinforce or may actually contradict the intended message.

The process of interpretation consists of seeking to understand the implications of the other's actions for self, and results in the invocation of scripts and the imputation of roles for self and other. That the script may be inappropriate and the imputed role may not be the one that the other wishes to project does not immediately effect the process since, at this stage, it is merely a role to be tested out in the 'theatre of the mind' through the process of simulation or *rehearsal*.

The Rehearsal of Action

Rehearsal is the imaginative anticipation of action; the 'theatre in the head' of social life. It is made possible by the human capacity for the manipulation of symbols and the capacity for taking the role of others discussed above. As a symbol user the individual does not have to go through with the complete act on a trial-and-error basis. He can replace the act by a symbol and consider its consequence in a mental process.

B conducts a conversation with himself to determine the meaning of the behaviour of A and the scene he finds himself in. In the process of this interpretation B attributes or imputes a role to A and, by inference and a knowledge of expected complementary patterns, to himself. Through a process of simulation B tests out the implications of A's assumed role and its consequence for him. Part of the test is the improvisation, the extempore performance of a role for himself which may or may not be in line with that imputed by A's behaviour. In effect he tries on a few pieces of behaviour and tests them for fit. He can simulate the situation several stages into the potential or alternative futures. This may mean a form of mental chess not only of the straightforward kind of 'if I do this, he will do that' but of the more machiavellian kind 'if I do this it may lead him to think that I wish to do such and such. Once he has swallowed that I can do. . . .'

Simulation, as conceived by Mead, requires the skills of a playwright, a director, actors, and an audience. The 'self' combines all of these in itself. As creator the self determines how best to structure events and performances to maintain its integrity; it also acts, as we have seen, so as to impute roles and motives to other actors. As director or producer of the drama, the self stages the performance in the 'theatre in the head', the place where the potential real-life drama is rehearsed and polished, its out-of-town try-out, as it were. As actor, the self imaginatively performs his own role and that of others, and as audience the self watches and critically evelutes the rehearsal. Throughout this procedure, the actor-dramatist-director-critic is aware of the relationship between his simulation or rehearsal and the theatre of social relations. He is aware that other performers are involved in similar simulations and that, therefore, he will need to accommodate their texts as well as his own. As the interaction proceeds he, and they, constantly revise, rewrite and rehearse their activities (Lyman and Scott, 1975).

In effect the actor indulges in a number of dry runs, dress rehearsals simulating his own behaviour, reactions to it, and so on. These dress rehearsals are clearly related to both definitions and action. He who defines things pessimistically is unlikely to rehearse a course of action, which departs radically from such definitions, and therefore he selects actions which tend to confirm these definitions. On the basis of audience and critical response to his rehearsal, B now dramatizes, expresses, and acts out what he takes to be his part in the unfolding drama of social interaction. His behaviour now becomes part of the scene for A and the cycle begins another spiral which repeats and repeats until the interaction is terminated.

Figure 2 illustrates the essential elements of a dyadic interaction. Much simplified, it depicts the steps leading up to performance by each social actor. Each actor places his or her interpretations upon the scene with which he is confronted; if they agree or have sufficient overlap for it not to matter, then the interaction can proceed. If, on the other hand, they have radically different interpretations, if they are seeking to invoke divergent scripts, the interaction will not proceed smoothly.

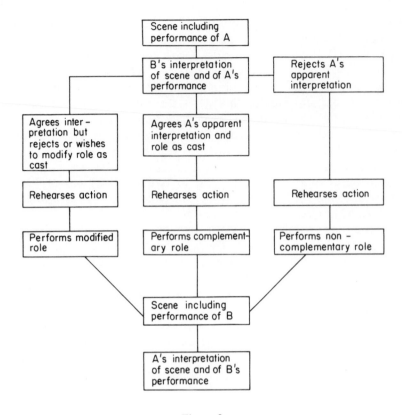

Figure 2

The diagram and the discussion reemphasizes the point that was made in the opening paragraphs of the chapter; that interaction is a seamless web. Each action can be seen as both a response and an initiative.

While analytically it is possible to separate the processes we must not allow the serial nature of our exposition to distort the fact that we have a process whereby presentation of behaviour by A *simultaneously* implies a role for B and the very act of construing that by B presupposes three things: a role for A, a role for B, and the joint action that is to arise by the articulation of these two roles. Thus the act of interpreting, of construing A's action, is inseparable from the process of simultaneously construing a potential response. The act of interpretation, the invocation of a particular situational script, is thus critical to the development of interaction; inability to put oneself into the role of the other is a crucial factor in the failure to fit lines of action to the other. 'Fundamentally, action on the part of a human being consists of taking account of various things that he notes and forging a line of conduct on a basis of how he interprets them . . .' (Blumer, 1969).

Summary

This chapter and the previous one have been concerned with some of the basic features of social interaction, the process by which social actors may be seen to relate to their own minds or the minds of others: 'the process, that is, in which individuals take account of their own or other fellows' motives, needs, desires, means and wills, knowledge and the like' (Swanson, 1965). The process is at the very heart of organizing and of society itself. I have proposed that social actors come together with idiosyncratic but overlapping repertoires and act out what they each take to be the appropriate script for the scene in which they find themselves. In effect, each actor seeks to bring into play certain preferred personal scripts within that which he takes to be the appropriate situational script. Each initial move in a new interaction is an attempt to define reality. Reality for each social actor are the cues and signals experienced by him as relevant to locating himself and others and engaging in action (Ball, 1972). The act of locating himself and others is essentially a creative one; the social actor pays selective attention to aspects of the scene and mentally combines these in order to understand their implications for his own possible performances. In effect, he fashions or selects a script and a role for himself from the scene.

This fashioning of action, this shaping of a potential response, may be seen to occur primarily through the process I have termed *rehearsal of action*. Through rehearsal the social actor seeks to try on various roles for himself and others and to try out the various courses of action he sees open to him in the light of his interpretation of the setting. Functioning as a playwright, he may improvise in the theatre of his mind his own behaviour and that of others, may select or, occasionally, write, may direct and act out the various scripts, and almost simultaneously may act as audience and critic at the resultant mental dress rehearsal.

Once the individual actor acts, his behaviour becomes part of the scene for the other actors. So the cycle continues with each action being potentially subject to interpretation by the other actors, and so on.

I will conclude this chapter as I began it by asserting that however useful the model may be in understanding the dynamics of interaction it is not posed as a model of how everyday personal and situational scripts are maintained. On the contrary, I would argue that such scripts are marked by their lack of deliberation; indeed, they are characterized by a fusion of the process of interpretation, rehearsal, and performance. My case has been and is that interaction, however, may be conceived of strategically, and the ability to take this standpoint with regard to one's own performances is an important human attribute which, as I shall argue later, has profound implications for the practice of creating and changing relationships.

PART II

Organizations

'Human organizations are not biological organisms; they are social inventions.' (Bavelas, 1960)

Chapter 5

The Elements of Organizing

I make no apology for having devoted so much space to the discussion of the possible interaction between a pair of social actors, 'Ego' and 'Alter', since, for me, the process of interaction between these two (as between Beckett's two tramps Vladimir and Estragon) can be seen as a microcosm of other social collectivities. If, as is the case, I am interested in the processes by which such collectivities are created, maintained, and dissolved, I can gain some insight into them by paying heed to the properties to be found in the simplest form of dyadic interaction. There is a continuity between the processes which occur between Laurel and Hardy and those which occur in the boardroom of I.C.I., and between the behaviour of Vladimir and Estragon and members of Her Majesty's Government. The processes may be expressed through whatever props and people may be at hand, and although performances may vary they remain, in essence, the same processes.

What this amounts to, of course, is the denial of the utility of phrases such as 'organizational' behaviour—and 'group behaviour'. The processes of interpretation and performance which constitute action in I.C.I. boardrooms and in cabinet offices are not unique; there is nothing specifically 'organizational' about them which distinguishes them from processes occurring between courting couples, knockabout comedians, members of a family, or participants in a charabanc outing. Encounters within organizations and groups resemble encounters elsewhere. Performances are performances and though the form (melodrama, tragedy, black comedy, etc.) may be shaped by the particular setting in which it unfolds (an I.C.I. board meeting is not, in most circumstances, similar to a charabanc outing); nonetheless, the performance still unfolds with a regularity and similarity of process which transcends the particular settings.

So far I have put forward a model of interaction based upon two assumptions about the nature of man: first, that he is in business to make sense of his world, to ascribe meaning to things and events and, second, that having ascribed such meaning he is concerned to express himself in order that his views shall be taken account of by others. This taking account of the views of others in orienting one's behaviour constitutes social interaction and is the stuff and fibre of all social activities.

Interaction occurs when Ego, seeking to reduce the equivocality of the world with which he is confronted and an opportunity to express behaviour which is dear to him, takes account of the behaviour of Alter and reaches an accommodation (however temporary) with him such that both derive some satisfaction from it. This accommodation, I have argued, is arrived at by a process of invocation of scripts, in turn dependent upon processes of self-presentation, altercasting, interpretation, rehearsal, and performance.

I have also argued that the daily round is not one of constant improvisation, tireless interpretation, and careful rehearsal, since much of what passes for everyday interaction has a taken-for-granted, well-rehearsed quality. Much of that which is deemed to constitute 'normal' interaction is non-problematic. Actors do not interact in a void and construct their social world *ab initio* on each and every occasion, but they approach interaction already influenced by past social experience and, to a marked extent, their choices (insofar as they are aware of them at all) are limited, if not determined, by the situational scripts most frequently utilized by other social actors past and present, in what are taken to be similar circumstances.

In this chapter I will seek to apply some of these ideas to behaviour within organizations. In particular I will give more attention to the nature of situational scripts and will speculate about the relationship between managerial role and the opportunity certain situational scripts afford for the indulgence of personal scripts and the exercise of strategic interactive capabilities. I will also be concerned with variations in the incidence of script imposition and will consider the idea of differential attachment to parts and scripts.

I have devoted some attention in the previous chapters to situational scripts but have not, so far, said very much about their origin. They have their origin in the patterns of mutual accommodation which arise as social actors seek to make their worlds more predictable by structuring associations. For each social actor, there is the possibility of reducing equivocality and satisfying his needs whenever he encounters another social actor. When some mutual accommodation is reached it may be in the interest of both parties to preserve it (depending, among other things, as I shall argue, upon the asymmetry of the relationship), and in such cases we have the elements of a situational script.

A situational script is created when a cycle of repetitive behaviours comes into being, a situation in which Ego regularly and usually constructs performances which are in line with Alter's interpretation of the scene and which in turn enables Alter to play parts which are in line with Ego's expectations.

The patterns of reciprocating behaviours lead directly to patterns of mutual expectations which gradually take on the character of a norm or set of norms which both Ego and Alter, and other social actors when faced with what they take to be similar situations, accept as binding upon themselves and as defining the particular conditions of their interactions. Thus, almost imperceptibly, interaction may be seen to move from relatively creative almost 'pure' examples of improvising performances such as occurs in highly novel situations, through circumstances in which performances are less extemporized to events in which the scripts and the parts have been stabilized and the patterns of expectation and behaviour are relatively clearly structured. In the terms used earlier, the movement is from the Second City Troupe to the ritual or classic theatre. I am not claiming that an organization is nothing more than a series of such situational scripts but I am saying that such behaviours do constitute the basic elements of organizing. Though arrived at from quite a different starting point my position is similar to (and clearly influenced by) that of Weick (1969:

'Interlocked behaviours are the basic elements that constitute any organization. They consist of repetitive, reciprocal, contingent behaviours that develop and are maintained between two or more actors. Each actor uses and is used by the other person for the accomplishment of activities which neither alone could accomplish.'

Thus organizing can be seen as the process of making, maintaining, and dissolving relationships and the organization, at any one time, as consisting of a network of such relationships which, in turn constitute the basis of situational scripts.

Situational Scripts and Improvisation

As implied above, some interlocked behaviours are more constraining than others. Some performances within organizations are characterized by a degree of improvisation not usually found elsewhere. Martin (1956) found in his study of what people do in an industrial plant that the staff foremen appeared

'to function almost completely in terms of alternatives which are ready-made and enduring—given in the form of rules. In the words of one division superintendent "Once the foremen decide that something has to be done, the rest is pretty well a matter of course—what they do and how." Action is here almost "ministerial", in that the basic question is whether or not a specific situation warrants evoking a particular rule. At the other extreme, the works manager frequently encounters situations in which the alternatives must be constructed. To illustrate, the works manager had received instructions from his superior to reduce costs. While the general direction is clear, here was a situation in which the various possible alternatives were not given. They had to be constructed. Formulations of these alternatives were based upon cues provided by production and cost data. The "how", however, had to be developed and worked out. In between these two extremes, the division superintendent and department foreman levels were concerned with decision situations of a mixed form.'

Some scripts have the characteristics of classic drama; every word, every gesture, every action clearly articulated, carefully directed, well rehearsed, and critically monitored. Frederick 'Speedy' Taylor (1911) provides us with a vivid illustration of how such classical situational scripts are constructed:

'The task before us, then, narrowed itself down to getting Schmidt to handle 47 tons of pig iron per day and making him glad to do it. This was done as follows. Schmidt was called out from among the gang of pig-iron handlers and talked to somewhat in this way: "Schmidt, you are a high-priced man?"
"Vell, I don't know vat you mean."
"Oh yes you do. What I want to know is whether you are a high-priced man or not."
"Vell, I don't know vat you mean."

60

"Oh, come now, you answer my questions. What I want to find out is whether you are a high-priced man or one of these cheap fellows here. What I want to find out is whether you want to earn $1.85 a day or whether you are satisfied with $1.15, just the same as all these cheap fellows are getting."

"Did I vant $1.85 a day? Vas dot a high-priced man? Vell, yes, I vas a high-priced man."

"Oh, you're aggravating me. Of course you want $1.85 a day—everyone wants it! You know perfectly well that has very little to do with your being a high-priced man. For goodness' sake answer my questions, and don't waste any more of my time. Now come over here. You see that pile of pig iron?"

"Yes."

"You see that car?"

"Yes."

"Well, if you are a high-priced man, you will load that pig-iron on that car tomorrow for $1.85. Now do wake up and answer my question. Tell me whether you are a high-priced man or not."

"Vell—did I get $1.85 for loading dot pig-iron on dot car tomorrow?"

"Yes, of course you do, and you get $1.85 for loading a pile like that every day right through the year. That is what a high priced man does, and you know it just as well as I do."

"Vell, dot's all right. I could load dot pig-iron on the car tomorrow for $1.85, and I get it every day, don't I?"

"Certainly you do—certainly you do."

"Vell den, I was a high-priced man."

"Now, hold on, hold on. You know just as well as I do that a high-priced man has to do exactly as he's told from morning to night. You have seen this man here before, haven't you?"

"No, I never saw him."

"Well, if you are a high-priced man, you will do exactly as this man tells you tomorrow, from morning till night. When he tells you to pick up a pig and walk, you pick it up and you walk, and when he tells you to sit down and rest, you sit down. And what's more, no back talk. Now a high-priced man does just what he's told to do, and no back talk. Do you understand that? When this man tells you to walk, you walk; when he tells you to sit down, you sit down, and you don't talk back at him. Now you come on to work here tomorrow morning I'll know before night whether you are really a high-priced man or not." (From pp. 44–47 in *Scientific Management* by Frederick Winslow Taylor. Copyright 1947 by Harper & Row, Publishers, Inc. Reprinted by permission of the publisher.)

He also provides us with some rules for the formulation of such scripts:

'The management must think out and plan the work in the most careful and detailed way, demanding of the worker not to seek to increase production by his own *initiative*, but to perform punctiliously the orders given down to their slightest detail.' (Friedman, 1961)

Taylor's prescription is such as to constrain the lower-level employee from writing and performing his own scripts. Such creative work is to be regarded as the prerogative of the manager; the employee must be content to play the part as presented to him. Taylor's presentation of self and that of many other managers is such as to cast the Schmidts of this world into a range of very narrow roles, aspects of which have been drawn up with what amounts to ritualistic precision. What is more, the director or his surrogate is to be present to ensure that the parts are played correctly and in accordance with the detailed stage directions.

Not only is his part to be written for him his every gesture subject to check and direction, but his relations with other social actors are to be prescribed. Close coordination of activities has to be imposed either by scripts, 'routines or rules which constrain action . . . into paths consistent with those taken by others in the interdependent relationship', or by 'the establishment of schedules for the interdependent units by which their actions may then be governed' (Thompson, 1967). There is no room for extemporization here, since it is clearly thought to be unnecessary. As Blau and Scott (1963) note, 'a free flow of suggestions and criticisms' (in my terms, less closely scripted behaviour) facilitates problem solving but 'impedes coordination'. Since, by definition, in lower-level jobs problems are scripted out as each 'whiff' (each contingency) has been considered by the scriptwriter—the manager—there is no need for extemporization, and close attention can therefore be devoted to coordination.

There are, of course, some qualifications to be made to this outline, not the least being that the opportunity to write scripts for others is crucially related not only to interpersonal skills at casting others into subordinate roles but also to power and to the expectations each party brings to the interaction from elsewhere. Although Taylor's interaction with Schmidt took place at the turn of the century, Taylor was forced to acknowledge that it was, even by standards then prevailing, 'rough talk'. It is doubtful whether such a script could be so readily constructed in many contemporary circumstances. I shall consider aspects of power and notions of competing interpretations shortly; for the moment I want to stay with the ideas of situational scripts.

It would be misleading to leave the reader with the impression that all situational scripts are as closely prescribed and as tightly monitored as that in which Schmidt and Taylor appear. The notion of situational scripts does not require that one actor dominates nor that one actor writes all the parts; it simply holds that in many circumstances there is a sequence of events, a shape to the performance, which is relatively predictable and relatively enduring. Taylor is attemping to construct such a situation, seeking, that is, to create a situational script such that whenever Schmidt is confronted by tons of pig iron he knows how to perform not only towards the pig iron but also towards the supervisor.

In a similar fashion situational scripts for preparing budgets, making plans, holding meetings, interviewing candidates, appraising people, relating to other departments, claiming expenses, doing research, making presentations, and so on, have evolved within any particular organization.

Thus I know, in general, what to expect from business meetings, not only because I have experienced such meetings in my own organization but because I have observed references to such meetings from the media and from colleagues and have developed ideas from abstractions I have made from other kinds of meetings. (Indeed, even before the days of the immortal Schmidt, Henry Martyn Robert took stock of existing knowledge about the conduct of meetings, systematized it, and produced a script, Robert's Rules of Order, which still has a wide influence.) I know the roles to be expected and the general sequence of events to be followed.

I know that on entering the room I have to locate a seat (in some circumstances even seating has become a matter of routine) and move to it. It is not usual to remain standing at the door, though it may be expected of a new member of the team that he hovers until introduced and invited to sit. My experience has taught me where it is appropriate to sit and should there be an obstruction to completing that act (what if there is no chair or what if there is someone else in my place?), I have learned the appropriate alternative performances (acquire a chair from elsewhere, ask the secretary to acquire one, turf the incumbent out of my chair, or glare at him and sit elsewhere).

The situational script probably proceeds along the lines of some desultory chat to be followed by the chairman of the meeting calling us to order and outlining the agenda or, should it have been previously circulated, proceeding directly to item one. If the chairman is not the most senior person present the script may require that he who is the most senior be deferred to and events will not move forward until he signals his readiness. There may be 'whiffs' for this stage of events also: what if the chairman doesn't call us to order? Coughing and pointedly looking at the clock may be appropriate or phrases such as 'I have another meeting at 10.30' may be utilized. In some circumstances direct questions of the order 'Shall we get on with it?' may even be acceptable.

Situational scripts are the product of repeated association with the situations involved in such scripts. Not only do I learn what to do and how to play my part but I also learn what is not considered to be appropriate behaviour. For example, the situational script of meetings may require me to pay attention to the discussion, but the whiff 'What if I am bored, angry or distraught?' is often only to be answered in terms of 'keep your mouth shut'. Business meetings are considered not to be the appropriate settings for displays of emotion, since the convention is one of rational performance and anything which may be thought to detract from that is to be discouraged:

'To the extent that individuals dedicate themselves to the value of rationality and getting the job done, they will tend to be aware of and emphasize the rational, intellective aspects of the interactions that exist in an organization and to suppress the interpersonal and emotional aspects, especially those that do not seem to be relevant to achieving the task. For example, one frequently hears in organizations "Let's keep feelings out of the discussion" or "Look here, our task today is to achieve objective X and not to get emotional". (This excerpt from 'On Organizations of the Future' by Chris Argyris is reprinted from *Sage Professional Papers in Administrative and Policy Studies*, Volume 1, Part 2 (1973) p. 13, by permission of the Publisher, Sage Publications, Inc. (Beverly Hills/London).)

Argyris' (1973) observation is interesting and confirms in fact that which I have said about the situational script of many forms of business meeting. However, in meetings where the script is really taken for granted—is, indeed, a familiar situational script—one is struck by the frequency with which one does *not* hear 'Let's keep feelings out of the discussion'. In such circumstances the script has a naturalness about it which precludes the raising of such issues.

However constraining the situational script of the business meeting, it does provide more opportunity for idiosyncratic performance than does the script within which many low-level employees operate. Simply because 'the overall responsibility of the organization cannot be broken down into fairly routine specialized tasks' (Blau and Scott, 1963), the manager is accorded an opportunity to develop and play a wider range of parts than is his lower-level counterpart. Two other factors affect the degree of strategic interaction manifested by any members of an organization; the nature of the job and the size of the organization.

Size affects situational scripts in the sense that the larger the number of people involved in the situation the greater the number of interactions and interpretations that have to be accommodated. The analysis of interaction in the previous chapter was confined to pairs of social actors and, even given this restriction, a considerable amount of information was potentially available to each of them in interpreting the scenes with which they were confronted. With more than two participants the sheer amount of information that needs processing to permit interpretation is greatly increased.

As the amount of information increases so the likelihood of accommodation decreases, since an increase in the numbers of the participants to a particular encounter carries with it the possibility of a greater number of competing interpretations and a resulting difficulty in agreeing upon any one as being appropriate or viable.

Size may also involve heterogeneity and may thus exacerbate the issue of competing interpretations: the more homogeneous the group—all similar, say, in terms of departmental affiliation, type of education, language, race, sex, and so on—the more interpretations are likely to be drawn from a similar stock of knowledge. Conversely, the greater the diversity the less likely the common stock of knowledge and shared experience and the more likely divergent interpretations.

Size may also affect the extent to which members of a particular organization are structurally segregated from one another. In the small organization, the managing director may know each of his employees and have an easy familiarity with each and every one of them based upon years of shared experience. In large organizations, however, the easy and intimate familiarity which may mark such encounters (they may also be rigid and distant, but nonetheless scripted) are less likely to be found, and the less the previous contact the greater will be the potential ambiguity of the scene. Social actors who are not well known are actors whose interpretations and performances are less predictable, thus rendering more problematic my interpretations and my actions.

The key feature here is that of potentially competing interpretations of the scene; the greater the number of actors, the more varied their backgrounds and intentions, the less usually encountered, the greater the potential diversity of interpretation, and thus the more likely that strategic rather than routine performance will be called into being (Lofland, 1976).

The manager is much more likely to be evolved in the kinds of interactions mentioned above than is the lower-level operative. He is more involved in meetings, often with people from departments other than his own and he, more often than the lower-level operative, has occasion to meet with a cross-section of the organization's employees. Above all, the manager is more likely to be involved in situations which involve competing definitions because his job is to do with people rather than with products, as Mintzberg (1973) confirms:

'Unlike other workers, the manager does not leave the telephone or the meeting to get back to work. Rather these contacts *are* his work. The ordinary work of the organization—producing a product, undertaking research, even conducting a study or writing a report—is seldom undertaken by its manager.'

Contracts and relationships are his work, and while many are routine and well scripted others are not, as Martin (1956) in his study of managerial decision making indicates:

'The social world of the works manager is one characterized by a multiplicity of superordinate and subordinate relationships, which are to a considerable degree indirect in nature and extending to members of out-groups. Hence there is a greater probability of uncertainty in anticipating how others will act.'

It is clear that the process by which the manager learns to play his parts in his scripts differs considerably from that by which the lower-level employee is expected to acquire his role. The former's learning is often the product of a lengthy period of professionalization and organizational socialization, whereas the latter's role is the product of a fairly short period of training and induction. It is equally clear that the scripts with which the manager is likely to become involved leave considerably more room for strategic interaction than does the script imposed upon the Schmidts of this world, a fact which has led Drucker (1954) to declare:

'The manager has the task of creating a true whole that is larger than the sum of its parts, a productive entity that turns out more than the sum of resources put into it. One analogy is the conductor of a symphony orchestra, through whose effort, vision and leadership individual instrumental parts that are so much noise by themselves become the living whole of music. But the conductor has the composer's score; he is only the interpreter. The manager is both composer and conductor.'

This is, in most situations, an overestimation of the manager's ability to write his own scores or scripts, a fact which Carlson (1951) notes:

'Before we made the study, I always thought of a chief executive as the conductor of an orchestra, standing aloof on his platform. Now I am in some respects inclined to see him as the puppet in the puppet-show with hundreds of people pulling the strings and forcing him to act in one way or another.'

Carlson's views, in turn, are an overestimation of the degree to which the manager's actions are constrained. There are circumstances in which performances must be constructed and there are circumstances within which his options are tightly circumscribed. Many of the manager's actions may be seen as falling between these two extremes and may also be seen as circumstances within which his performance is influenced by professional training.

The foregoing outline of ideas about the degree of strategic interaction likely to occur at different organizational levels is derived from the theoretical notions outlined in the previous chapters. It suggests that behaviour in organizations may be conceptualized along a scale ranging from scripts which are to be rigidly performed to those in which a much greater range of expression and strategic performance is possible. The greater part of behaviour within organizations consists of situational scripts which have been evolved to deal with circumstances, and most of the performances observable within organizations relate to such scripts whether such performances result from imposed scripts or from professionally acquired ones.

Script Imposition and Attachment

As was indicated in the discussion of the Taylor/Schmidt interaction, behaviour within organizations may be considered in terms of the extent to which the relationship is symmetrical with regard to the ability to influence the interpretations each actor places upon a particular scene. The ability to persuade another actor of a particular interpretation may be related to interpersonal skill; the con-man, the magician, the politician, and the salesman are all, to a greater or lesser extent, skilled in persuading us to accept their interpretations. In other circumstances, notably in institutions and organizations, interpretations are more likely to be constrained by unequal access to information and by general scripts or ideologies concerning the rights of others to impose their interpretations. Taylor is able to impose a script upon Schmidt in part because (1) he has access to information that is denied the latter which confers upon him the ability to quote costs and quantities and, perhaps more importantly, (2) Schmidt, both in his extra organizational roles and his experience with the particular organization, may have been led to believe that it is *legitimate*, that it is part of the natural order of events, for supervisors and managers to behave in the fashion advanced by Taylor. Thus he acknowledges Taylor's power to write, cast, and direct the dramas in which he will appear.

Like Sam Gerridge in Robertson's play 'Caste' (1956) he may think that we should each look to the differences in our stations:

'Sam: I mean what I say. People should stick to their own class. Life's a railway journey, and mankind's a passenger—first class, second class, third class. Any person found riding in a superior class to that for which he has taken his ticket will be removed at the first station stopped at, according to the bye-law of the company.'

To the extent what Schmidt accepts that 'life's a railway journey' and to the extent that he desires the benefits of interstructured behaviour and is unable to obtain them with equal or more satisfaction elsewhere, he will continue to interact with Taylor and raise no questions in so doing.

The introduction of the qualifications, the conditions under which Schmidt will continue to associate with Taylor, however, draws attention to another feature of the model which has implications for the study of processes occurring within organizations. If we take the opposite line from that adopted in the previous paragraph and assume for the moment that Schmidt does not accept that we each have been allotted separate stations and should keep to them, and if we further assume that he is aware of and does not like the role of 'stupid immigrant' into which he has been cast Taylor, what then may ensue? Obviously if the encounter or association is not one that is likely to meet some of his expectations he can decline to participate: he can withdraw from the interaction. However, if it is further assumed that his participation is involuntary (he has been, say, conscripted into the army, has been convicted of assault upon a previous supervisor or has been committed to an asylum by his workmates) or that, which is more likely to be the case, he cannot achieve even minimal satisfaction of his needs elsewhere, what then? My contention is that Schmidt is likely to interpret such scenes as ones in which he must act out the part of the stupid immigrant; in effect, he recognizes that he is nothing more than a bit player, but since it is the only play in town he has little choice but to take it in.

In such circumstances, his attachment to the script as written by Taylor may be less than complete and his performance of the role for which he has been cast may be carried out with less than total enthusiasm. He may even signal throughout his performance that he is miscast, that he is carrying it out under duress; the armed forces have recognized such a category of performance and make the more obvious manifestation of it indictable offences under the heading 'dumb insolence'. Less colloquially, the behaviour has been awarded the little of 'role-distance' by Goffman (1961). A person achieve role-distance when he can and does perform a role passably, but with a certain disdain for the role itself. In the one set of circumstances, as I have shown, Schmidt may identify with the role as cast and may even regard it as an appropriate expression of his view of himself or, given other factors affecting his interpretation, he may regard the role as something which has to be performed at a distance from his idealized view of how he would like to see himself acting in the particular interaction.

The point I am wishing to make is that both acceptance of the role and the playing of the role with a degree of distance are, in the case of Schmidt, influenced by the different images that he may hold of the place of authority outside the organization. Less specifically, the images of behaviour, the expectations, and roles that each and every actor brings to the organization influence the meanings that actors accord to different scripts and hence their attachments to particular roles. Which is not to deny that attachment, expectations, and roles may not be, in turn, influenced by the actors' experience within the organization. Schmidt's interaction with Taylor may develop so that it is brought more in line with some of his needs and, to the extent that it is, will influence extraorganizational interpretations and scripts with which he is associated and the degree of attachment with which he plays his part within the organization. What is more, Schmidt's needs, like those of any other social actor, may change as a result of the interaction within the organization. All of which serves to remind us that attachments to an organization 'reflect the meanings which those concerned bring in from the wider society *and* the finite provinces of meaning specific to the organization' (Silverman, 1970).

Thus organizations may be conceptualized as a series of situational scripts which may be more or less open to the construction of extempore performances, a feature which may be relative to occupational categories, size, and hierarchial levels; they may also be seen as collectivities in which, depending upon the interpretations brought to them and the meanings which arise as they interact, social actors are more or less attached to the situational scripts.

Some Further Implications

Beyond all else, organizations may be conceptualized as collectivities which are dependent upon the meanings and purposes which individuals bring to them from the wider society and, hence, as collectivities in which there is no necessary consensus of interpretation and purpose. Each social actor may play his part in the situational script, but his purpose in so doing and the degree of attachment he has to his performance may differ from that of other social actors party to the script. To the extent that his expectations are not met or to the extent that they change he will seek to bring the script more into line with them, just as will the other actors. Thus meaning and performance may be seen as a continuous process of bargaining and temporary accommodation between individuals and groups. Order may thus be seen as that which is improvised, maintained, and dissolved by the interpretation and performance of the social actors involved. That which is taken for granted, unquestioned, part of the natural order of events is nothing if not constantly reaffirmed in the interpretation and actions of the social actors associated with it. Once the cues are questioned, the parts and lines subjected to scrutiny, the present order may be changed; where there is no questioning, no scrutiny, the script is performed normally and order is sustained.

Summary

Seen in the light of the model presented earlier, social relations within organizations arise out of the interaction of the social actors and are informed by varying interpretations as to what constitutes appropriate behaviour.

Order may be seen to the result of a series of temporary accommodations–joint efforts to reduce equivocality and secure the satisfactory performance of a minimum role for each actor. What obtains in any given circumstance will be the outcome of a mutual accommodation which itself may be jointly negotiated or the result of the relative capacity of different actors to impose their interpretations upon others and to act so as to cast others in complementary roles.

Chapter 6

Boring Stories and Exciting Dramas

According to Schank and Abelson (1977), a situational script is a 'boring little story'. They hold this view since, by definition, such scripts have been evolved to handle stylized everyday situations and, therefore, tend not to be subject to much change. Situational scripts certainly constrain novel performance but, perhaps more importantly, they constrain us in such a way that we consider our performance to be 'only natural'; the power of the situational script lies in its quality of common sense. Our performance and that of others is to be expected–part of the natural order of events. No other performance is conceivable; what we do and how we do it is taken to be 'human nature'.

This is so because the situational script reflects the shared stock of knowledge which, in effect, consists of the received notions about what constitutes appropriate performance in different contexts. Taylor knows how he ought to behave as a manager and he knows how Schmidt ought to behave towards him. Taylor knows, or thinks he does, what motivates Schmidt's performance and knows that Schmidt will see his, Taylor's, performance as in the interests of both himself and Schmidt.

Taylor's interpretation of the situational script is confirmed by the actions of Schmidt who accepts the role as cast by Taylor and, in so doing, reinforces Taylor's self-presentation and, by derivation, Taylor's own view of himself and his actions. As Taylor and Schmidt continue to perform their respective roles the pattern of interstructured behaviour which results becomes a situational script which takes the mutually elaborated roles to be the 'natural order'. In this way the roles of manager and worker are defined and, as they pass into common usage, it is no longer even noticed that generations of Schmidts and Taylors imbibe the assumptions upon which they are based. 'After all, isn't it commonsense that those with brains should do the planning and organizing, and those with brawn should do the physical work?'

Once a situational script has been established, strong impulses come into play to maintain its essentially boring nature. Habit and the power of tradition combine to suppress any tendency to deviation; the sacred script is to be protected and performances of an almost ritual character are to be encouraged, even when we are no longer sure what scripts they sustain. Morrison (1966) provides a beautiful illustration which I cannot resist quoting:

'In the early days of the last war when armaments of all kinds were in short supply, the British, I am told, made use of a venerable field piece that had come down to them from previous generations. The honorable past of this light artillery stretched back, in fact, to the Boer War. In the days of uncertainty after the fall of France, these guns, hitched to trucks, served as useful mobile units in the coast defence. But it was felt that the rapidity of fire could be increased. A time-motion expert was, therefore, called in to suggest ways to simplify the firing procedures. He watched one of the gun crews of five men at practice in the field for some time. Puzzled by certain aspects of the procedure, he took some slow motion pictures of the soldiers performing the loading, aiming and firing routines.

When he ran these pictures over once or twice, he noticed something that appeared odd to him. A moment before the firing, two members of the gun crew ceased all activity and came to attention for a three-second interval extending throughout the discharge of the gun. He summoned an old colonel of the artillery, showed him the pictures, and pointed out the strange behaviour. What, he asked the colonel, did it mean. The colonel too, was puzzled. He asked to see the pictures again. "Ah", he said when the performance was over, "I have it. They are holding the horses."

This story, true or not, and I am told that it is true, suggests nicely the pain with which the human being accommodates himself to changing conditions. The tendency is apparently involuntary and immediate to protect oneself against the shock of change by continuing in the presence of the altered situation the familiar habits, however incongruous, of the past.' (Reprinted from *Men, Machines and Modern Times* by E. E. Morrison by permission of the M.I.T. Press, Cambridge, Massachusetts.)

It is not simply a matter of habit and tradition that social actors call upon in maintaining situational scripts and well-rehearsed performances. The scripts have evolved in order to meet the needs of some, if not all, of the social actors involved in them, and those who derive satisfaction from them are likely to seek to sustain them rather than to disrupt them. Situational scripts arise in conditions of equivocality and represent adaptations to that equivocality, and the fact that they are 'boring little stories' may be welcomed by those who see the social world as containing too much that is unpredictable and far from routine. Beyond all else, however, situational scripts are resistant to change since, to the extent that the social actors are attached to their roles, they will consider them important aspects of their self-concepts and a change in the role or the 'natural order' of events entails a change in the way of seeing the self which may pose a threat to the person's sense of wholeness or integrity. The conservatism of situational scripts is due to both their nature as boring adaptations to equivocality and to the nature of the attachment individual social actors have for them.

Nonetheless, widespread though fixity, conservatism, and the social persistence of situational scripts may be, such features only obtain to the extent that social actors continuously perform according to the scripts. Situational scripts may be handed down from generation to generation and may actually be elaborated before our eyes, as in the Schmidt/Taylor interaction, but they only recur to the extent that the social actors play their parts time and time again. Without reaffirmation in action the script does not exist. 'The realisation of the drama,' as Berger and Luckmann (1966) point out, 'depends upon the reiterated performance of its prescribed roles by living actors. The actors embody the roles and actualise the drama by presenting it on the given stage. Neither drama nor institution exists empirically apart from this recurrent realisation.'

The situational script for a contemporary Schmidt and Taylor is now more than likely to be markedly different to that which was played out at the turn of the century. I can imagine it proceeding along the following lines:

'The task before us, then, narrowed itself down to getting Schmidt to handle 12 tons of pig iron per day and of being able to meet his demands for extra payments for so doing. This was done as follows. Schmidt was called out from among the gang of pig-iron handlers around the tea urn and talked to somewhat in this way:

"Look, Bill, we've got a bit of a problem."

"Oh yes."

"Yes, I wonder if you could help resolve.it."

"Depends doesn't it?"

"On what?"

"On what the problem is and how much it's worth to the management to solve it."

"Look, Bill, it's no use taking that line. We are in the muck up to here and you know it. The old man wants us to get out of it by getting productivity up and unless we do there could be real trouble, short-time, lay-offs. . . ."

"Are you threatening something Mr Taylor?"

"No, don't pull that one, Bill. I'm just putting you in the picture. Just spelling out what it's all about to you. . . ."

"That's all right then. Any question of short-time, lay-offs, redundancies is a matter for the unions, not for the likes of you and me to sort out. So's productivity for that matter. . . ."

"I know that, Bill, I know that. But a word from you in the right ear you know. . . , Just a matter of getting up to somewhere around twelve tons a day."

"Twelve!"

"Yes, twelve."

"Impossible. Bloody impossible. What do you think we are, bloody fork-lift trucks or somat?

"Look, Bill, be fair. Don't bugger me around. You know it can be done. Christ, I've a job to do the same as you, don't bloody crucify me."

"Might be able to sell 'em ten tons. No more."

"I'll settle for that. So long as there's some improvement. We can't go on like this. . . ."

"Have to talk to the Union about rates, mind, you can't expect ten tons without paying for it." '

There can be no doubt that even if the above script is thought to show a degree of exaggeration and artistic licence not found in everyday life (and I'm not accepting that it does), the relationship and the language of interaction between the Schmidts and Taylor of industry have changed over the years.

The Dynamics of Change

In both of the interactions involving Schmidt and Taylor situational scripts are operating; both parties know the approximate course events will take and both know how to talk to each other such that each gets something out of the encounter (however minimal that may be). Thus the script for the interaction is maintained by the nature of the interaction itself. It follows that the script may also be changed through the process of interaction. Indeed, we have an example of attempted change when Taylor wields the big stick of short-time and lay-offs which results in Schmidt rapidly bringing him back to his part: 'Are you threatening something, Mr Taylor?' Threats are clearly not to be tolerated as part of this particular situational script, however acceptable they may have been in the past: 'We'll see if you are a high-paid man or not.'

Change occurs in situational scripts for a number of reasons. First, as I have indicated at length, social actors may bring competing interpretations to bear upon the scene in which they find themselves and, what is more, they may change these interpretations in the course of the interaction. Such interpretations are themselves influenced by the general stock of scripts available and the widely held assumptions about how various social actors should interrelate. Thus at the turn of the century there may have been more widespread agreement about the superiority of management and the consequent ligitimacy of their authority than is the case now (such an agreement itself would be based upon consensus about wider issues such as social class, the rights of capitalists, and so on). As these wider views change so those of the participants to a particular encounter may change (and, of course, vice versa) and adjustments become necessary. Adjustments only occur if the variations in interpretation or the wish to prosecute an original interpretation or role results in a difference in attachment to a particular situational script and if there is some shift in power which makes an adjustment possible. Accommodations not based upon the imposition of an interpretation by one party or the other are marked by a series of mutual adjustments to changing interpretations. The situational scripts based upon Berger and Luckmann's (1966) principle of 'He who has the bigger stick has the better chance of imposing his definitions' changes as the result of the other parties acquiring larger sticks or as a result of them depriving the other of his stick.

Situational scripts embody the institutionalized interpretations about the likely performances of self and others in a particular setting and are essential to the conduct of social life. They express the lines of action which all social actors party to them tend to accept for the time being, either because they are deeply attached to them or because they can do nothing for the moment to alter them. To the extent that interpretations and personal scripts change and to the extent that any particular social actor (or group of social actors) experiences low attachment to the situational script, he may be more or less continually involved in seeking to alter it; to the extent that his interpretations and personal scripts remain constant, the social actor will seek to maintain the situational script in its current form.

The process of change can be illustrated by considering the interaction between our two familiar characters, Schmidt and Taylor, as it goes through a critical and awkward phase. The original situational script, it will be recalled, appeared to be based upon some clear roles to be enacted—Taylor the thinker, planner, and organizer of the work and Schmidt the doer, the machine-like shifter of material, and obedient servant of his master's voice. For a time and for many reasons, Schmidt may fall in with the scripts assigned and act out the part of 'stupid immigrant'; if all of his experience within and without the plant combine to reinforce this identity and, unlikely though it may be, if he is not aware of any stigma attaching to such a part, he will continue to perform in accordance with Taylor's wishes. If, however, in some other script (say a political one, an educational one, or a commercial one) he is not allotted the part of 'stupid immigrant' or if he becomes aware that physical work is less highly regarded than that which requires the exercise of intelligence, he may seek to change his work script such as to bring it more into line with his part in other, more valued, scripts.

Let us assume that Schmidt is no longer content to be cast in the role of non-thinking adjunct to a machine. By his actions he expresses the new image of himself, possibly by raising questions, possibly by initiating minor but obvious changes in the way that he goes about loading the pig iron. In so doing he recasts Taylor's role since no longer is he accepting that Taylor (or his surrogate) is to define when he may sit, walk, or talk. In effect he is declaring by his actions: 'In this script I am taking more responsibility for my performance and you less.' It may happen that Taylor is unwilling to think of Schmidt and himself in these revised parts and cannot abandon the notions he has held heretofore. Thus he responds to the performance of Schmidt by replying brusquely to the questions (in the manner well caught in the extract quoted above) and forbidding the innovations. This may be the end of the attempted alteration, but it is more than likely that given the strength of Schmidt's competing interpretations, the attempt will be simply deferred to a later date. Relations between Schmidt and Taylor will be marked by a series of such attempts and such rebuffs. Eventually, either because Schmidt's position is strengthened or Taylor's weakened, Schmidt may win some degree of freedom for himself, only to have it wrested back from him as interpretation and power changes. And so the process repeats and repeats.

The nature of interaction is such that it may be characterized by successive mutual accommodation, each more or less temporary and each subject to reinterpretation, adjustment, change, or transformation. To paraphrase Berger and Pullsberg (1966), 'All situational scripts are precarious' in that they depend for their stability upon regular and relatively unvarying reaffirmation through performance in accordance with the lines. Departure from the lines, as it were, may signal a change in the actor's conception of his part and may lead to a revision of the script for all the actors involved.

Such revisions may be minor or quite substantial. The minor modifications are well captured by Moore (1962):

'Each comes, plays his part, moves on to other roles and is followed by another bit player to take his turn. Yet individuals do differ, to permit a little freedom to the man being shaped. A man never really leaves a position to his successor precisely as he received it from his predecessor. He will have added a little or subtracted a little from his duties, he will have changed direction at least slightly. . . .' (Reproduced by permission of Random House, Inc.)

Such additions, subtractions, and deviations in and of themselves do not constitute change of any significance. Indeed, they could be denied the attribute of change entirely if we follow Nisbet (1972) and define it as 'a succession of differences in time in a persisting identity'. A minor movement, a minor addition or subtraction, is unlikely to make a difference to the nature of the ongoing relationship between, say, the manager and the managed. A whole series of such minor modifications, however, may transform the relationship. There can be no doubt that there are differences over time in the persisting identity–the interstructured behaviour—of Schmidt and Taylor and, furthermore, it may be argued that such differences as now obtain are the result of numerous past modifications of and deviations from the previously accepted script.

Thus philosophies of management and personnel policy may *evolve*, not without difficulty and certainly not necessarily in a direct line, from those designed to increase the employee's productivity regardless of his social or intellectual well-being to those which, while still concerned with productivity, take account of his social and intellectual expectations. If they go beyond this to the point where the individual worker has a substantial say in issues relating to productivity and his social/intellectual needs, however gradually this point is arrived at, a substantial change in the relationship has occurred.

Thus some change in relationships and, hence, in behaviour within organizations may be explained as the product of a whole series of revisions in interpretation and performance, which in and of themselves may be relatively minor but cumulatively affect the persisting identity of the relationship.

Other changes may be characterized by substantial discontinuity. In such circumstances the script is not simply modified, the role not merely elaborated and developed. The script is torn up; new parts are cast and performed. Such dramatic shifts, though far from being the normal order of events, can be seen to occur and can be distinguished from those which arise from the gradual, cumulative process outlined above. Shakespeare, as always, captures the shift well in his depiction of the relationship between Othello and Desdemona:

'Othello: It gives me wonder great as my content
              To see you here before me. O my soul's joy!
              If after every tempest come such calms
              May the winds blow till they have waken'd death
              And let the labouring boat climb hills of seas
              Olympus-high and duck again as low
              As hell's from heaven. If I were now to die
              'Twere now to be more happy; for I fear
              My soul hath her content so absolute
              That not another comfort like to this
              Succeeds in unknown fate.
Desdemona: The heavens forbid
              But that our lives and comforts should increase
              Even as our days do grow.
Othello: Amen to that, sweet powers
              I cannot speak enough of this content:

It stops me here; it is too much joy.
And this, and this, the greatest discords to be

(They kiss.)
That e'er our hearts shall make.'

There are, however, far greater discords to come, such that later we find a substantial difference in the relationship:

'Desdemona: Alas, what ignorant sin have I committed?
Othello: Was this fair paper, this most goodly book
Made to write "whore" upon? What committed?
Committed! O thou public commoner!
I should make very forges of my cheeks
That would to cinders burns my modesty,
Did I but speak thy deeds. What committed!
Heaven stops the nose at it, and the moon winks:
The bawdy wind, that kisses all it meets,
Is hush'd within the hollow mine of earth
And will not hear it. What committed!
Impudent strumpet!
Desdemona: By heaven you do me wrong.'

Less poetically but more organizational in flavour is the following extract which captures well (even though I do say so myself) the gaping, slack-jawed impact a radical redefinition of the taken-for-granted world by a superior has upon his subordinates. Tom, who speaks first, is a very senior man from Chicago (headquarters of the parent chemical company). Mickey is the local manager of a cosmetics company (recently acquired by Crocodile, the chemical company) who has been drafted in from the parent company to manage alongside Tony, previously in sole charge of the cosmetic operation. Mike Thomson is from the headquarters of the cosmetic company in New York and, like both Tom and Mickey, originally a Crocodile man. Up to the point where we join them, the taken-for-granted world has been a Crocodile world—a world of systems, committees, and careful, protracted decision making.

TOM: *Roy, I don't think anyone will object to that for a moment. What bothers me though is the low level of our sights. The whole marketing plan which you outlined on Wednesday is so safe as to be bloody ridiculous. Many of us could make those figures even if we closed E.A.O. down tomorrow. It's a belt-and-braces approach . . . much too pessimistic. Its not what this business needs; we've got to get out after that bottom line. Go out and zap the profits, really zap them. We spend far too much of our time piddling about in cost-cutting exercises and not enough after the dollars . . . we've got to get up and go . . . really zap the profits. . . .*

MICKEY: *I agree with you 100 per cent Tom, but we don't spend all that time cutting down the costs; we're after the profits as well.*

TONY: *No! No! Mickey, that's not true and you know its not true. Look at all the time we have put in saving a few dollars here and there, when the market's just slipping away from us, just slipping away!*

MICKEY: *Oh! that's just not the way I see it. Crocodile has always been keen on keeping good control on things like salary, car costs, packaging, etc., that's the way Crocodile wants it. . . .*

MIKE: *Who says? What? . . . You say, New York says, Chicago says. That's who says. Everyone says.*

MIKE: *No Sir, we don't. We want the business to be managed successfully but we don't say that the best way of doing that is necessarily the Crocodile way. No one is New York told you to spend hour after hour of the day in group meetings. No one is New York told you to adopt the Crocodile personnel policies. Hell, in this business that in dangerous. Guys come and go in this industry, in one day and out the next. You just don't recruit for life as we do in Crocodile. No Sir, this is different and we have to manage it different. I am convinced that. . . .*

MICKEY: *Oh! come off it Mike, come off it. You were the guy slamming the system in a year or two back. And now . . . even now you spend 80 per cent of your time checking things out in Chicago . . . you're more of a Crocodile man than any of us.*

MIKE: *No Sir, that's not true. I'm Vice-President of a Cosmetics Company and that's a helluva lot different from being a Vice-President of a Chemical Company. It's my job to convince Crocodile of that, and that takes time. Eighty per cent of it at the moment. But your job is to manage the business in the most appropriate way, to buck the system where it doesn't fit and get after the bottom line, get after those profits. . . .*

MICKEY: *Let me get this straight. Am I hearing you properly? Are you saying that we don't need to spend time crossing all the Ts and dotting all the Is? That we don't need to be spending our time on personnel policies, car requisitions, territorial surveys. . . .*

MIKE: *Your job is to get out there and move the merchandise. . . .*

MICKEY: *Jeeezuz Christ. . . .*

What Mike is proposing is a dramatic shift in the reciprocity of perspectives, a bouleversement of the taken-for-granted world as to how this particular subsidiary should be managed. The incredulity of Roy's response is some indication of how non-negotiable the scene appeared to have been up to that point. Mike's intervention transforms the meaning of management or, to be more exact, provides the basis for a transformation or negotiation about the meaning of management.

Changes of the same type may be observed within organizations when the 'new broom sweeps clean'; the newly appointed manager makes a substantial number of changes of personnel and procedures and, in so doing, brings about a radical change in the situational script that has previously obtained.

Equally observable with organizations is the change in performance which is sought by reassigning tasks or by the creation of new agencies to accomplish that which is deemed not to have been well performed by the previous actors. George

Brown (1972) in his political memoirs, indicates that such ideas were behind the move in 1964 to set up a Department of Economic Affairs to take over some of the traditional functions of the Treasury:

'At Transport House we were already thinking of all kinds of ways of re-styling the Government.

Economic thinking was very much part of this, and at that stage there was a considerable body of opinion which held that economic policy in Britain was too much subordinated to the financial considerations of the Treasury. We were all (at least, most of us who were concerned with Labour Party policy) expansionists at heart, and we thought that the economy was being held back, that unemployment was being kept high, that all sorts of barriers were being erected to keep down industrial activity, by reason of the orthodox financial policy of the Treasury. Out of this kind of thinking grew the idea that it would be better to have an economic department which (as I always saw it) would be superior to the Treasury in determining the country's economic priorities.' (Reproduced by permission of Victor Gollancz Ltd and St. Martin's Press.)

The change in the relationship between Othello and Desdemona is of a different order to that of the change between Schmidt and Taylor, and the change in organization envisaged by George Brown is of a different nature to that which not only occurs but is encouraged in many major organizations—gradual, cumulative, change that is not calculated to upset too many applecarts. I am not suggesting that such movements occur suddenly and without preparation, that they are entirely novel and without precedent. I am simply stating that they are discontinuous and by this I mean that they are a rewriting and a recasting of the situational script which are difficult to account for in terms of the successive, mutual accommodations that have previously occurred within the script.

In sum I am proposing that there are two kinds of change. The first are those which occur gradually by the actions and interpretations of the social actors as they mutually accommodate and which have the quality of each stage of the relationship leading to the next stage. In this sense change can be seen to emanate from the conditions which precedes it. The other kind of change may be seen to be discontinuous with that which precedes it and is marked by either the social actors stepping outside the situational scripts and radically revising them or the script being rewritten by one or more social actors without the cooperation of the others.

It may not be reasonable to subsume discontinuous change under continuous change, but, as far as I am concerned, it is both possible and reasonable to see both varieties of change as explicable within the dramaturgical perspective. I have argued that situational scripts arise as social actors seek to reduce the essential equivocality of their worlds by interstructuring their performances. And I have further argued that such scripts as arise from these activities may have the character of 'boring little stories', with all the attributes of persistence and fixity, convention, routine, custom, and habit. Nonetheless, boredom is not total; differences in the persisting identities of relationships do occur over time and arise because the nature of interaction is such that it may be composed of a *temporary* accommodation of competing interpretations (or such interpretations may arise in the course of playing out situational scripts). The difference between continuous and discontinuous change lies in the actors' awareness of the strength of the competing interpretations. Conflicts of interpretations may be *relatively* minor and but dimly perceived by the actor: in Schmidt's case it may be that he wishes to change the value of his contribution, to be treated less as a machine and more of a human being. In such cases adjustment and accommodation may be possible while not disrupting entirely the nature of the situational script. In other cases competing interpretations may be relatively diverse and sharply perceived: Schmidt may come to see himself as exploited by Taylor and seek as a consequence to radically change the situational script.

Discontinuous change is often accompanied by a sense of crisis which as Nisbet (1972) notes is

'the common result when a way of behaviour long taken for granted by the participants comes for the first time into sharp and *perceived* conflict with some other way of behaviour, and with the values embodied in that other way of behaviour. What has been regarded as normal or as unavoidable, or even as consecrated into a sacred way, becomes, or can become, for the first time the object of critical attention.'

Attention is crucial to the conception of social change which is being outlined here. Without the social actor paying attention, without his awareness of a competing interpretation, differences will not arise. There may be, for example, a whole range of interpretations around as to what constitutes the woman's part in the family, but differences in particular situational scripts will only occur to the extent that the woman concerned is aware of a particular alternative interpretation and can either reach a new accommodation with her partner or can precipitate a crisis, such that a revision in the current accommodation is inevitable.

Logically, without recourse to a large stock of interpretations, the social actor has no possibility of effecting differences over time in the persisting identity of a particular relationship. It is impossible to understand the change in the relationship between Othello and Desdemona without recourse to the interpretations of Desdemona's actions Iago offers to Othello. Equally it is impossible to deal with the difference over time in the Schmidt/Taylor relationship without bringing into consideration the potential impact of technological, educational, industrial, and political scripts. In Great Britain, for example, the scenario for a 'just' society developed by the Labour Party, itself influenced by working men, has, arguably, had a major impact upon the interactions of those working men with their supervisors and employers. The impact has not been uniform; some workers may not have paid much attention to the particular ideology, some may reject it, some may interpret the situation as being unamenable to change, some may be influenced by competing ideologies, some may accord changes in their relationships low priority, and so on. There is no direct relationship between changes in the law, in political ideology, or anything else and changes in, say, relationships at work. Change occurs as the result of the social actors paying attention to the revised stock of scripts potentially available to them, thus giving them the possibility of revising the interpretations they put upon their interaction and, consequently (other things being equal), of effecting changes in it.

In sum, change may be defined as differences in a persisting identity over time and can be seen to be of two kinds: as the outcome of almost continuous, step-by-step, gradual adjustment and refinement of roles and scripts, and as that which may be characterized as much more exciting dramatic and sharply discontinuous with the previous situational script. The contrast lies between boring stories and exciting dramas. Both kinds of change are consistent with the basic dramaturgical model outlined in these pages, since the model propounds that actors may bring to the relationship (or may develop during it) competing interpretations as to the meaning of it and their part in it. The sharper the perceived competition and the less the attachment to the current roles as cast for him on the part of at least one of the parties to the relationship, the more likelihood there is of discontinuous change occurring.

The Limits to Organizational Change

Although both types of change can be observed in relations within organizations, discontinuous change is much less likely than that which occurs by gradual adjustment of the script from within. Crisis and heightened attention do not always result in fundamental change:

'History is filled with instances of attention failing to create a new mode of behaviour for a group of people and of the individual concerned lapsing back into the customary and habitual. It cannot be too greatly stressed that the moments in history are rare when, as the result of crisis, and some form of "attention" given the crisis by some group or by some elite or individual, a genuinely new way of life is the result. Much oftener, as I say, the consequence proves to be a kind of weathering of the crisis and then a regression to the familiar and traditional.' (Nisbet, 1972)

In one way, looking at events from a dramaturgical perspective, restoration of the status quo is to be expected; in another it is not. Theoretically, given that the actors' attention is focused upon some element which implies that a change in the ongoing script is appropriate, scripts should be capable of modification without too much trouble. Practically, of course, this is rarely the outcome. Change is nearly always confronted by strong forces holding it in check and sharply circumscribing the potential rewriting of the situational scripts.

The forces which limit the capacity of any given actor or group of actors to rewrite the script are, I believe, inherent to the model of interaction I have proposed, and are related to the assumption which informs interstructured behaviour—the reason for any situational script—to the fact of competing interpretations and, above all, to the casting and direction of the actors. At the risk of repetition I wish to reconsider some of these issues.

The Perceived Benefits of Reduced Equivocality

I have proposed earlier in this book that actors come together and indulge in joint action notably so as to have opportunity of satisfying their effectance or performance motives, but also so as to reduce the equivocality of the world, to effect closure, and to make events and encounters *relatively* predictable. The assumption made is similar to that proposed by Weick (1969):

'Assume that change rather than stability is the rule. People are continually exposed to streams of ongoing events (Schutz, 1967). If change is so continuous, it becomes difficult for a person to make sense of what is happening and to anticipate what will happen *unless* he is able to make some of these events recur. If a person wants to make the world more predictable, then he has to establish events which terminate and are repeated.'

Collective structure emerges to produce order and regularity and, thus, to reduce equivocality. At the organizational level such interstructured behaviour is often expressed as routines, as standard operating procedures, and as prescribed ways of behaving and interacting. Any change in the situational script, the pattern of interstructured behaviour, implies a movement away from stability and regularity and towards greater equivocality. He who would change things needs to show that the perceived benefits of the present script would not be lost in the new arrangement. This feature of interaction tends to favour the status quo; since there is an assumption that equivocality is reduced by joint action, some joint action is required, and what may be proposed may increase rather than reduce the present level of uncertainty. The logic of collective behaviour may thus have a conservative nature, a built-in inertia that maintains it as it is rather than a dynamic which constantly moves it forwards into the unknown. A fear of chaos and equivocality which in Hamlet's words

'... makes us rather bear these ills we have
Than fly to others that we know not of:
Thus conscience does make cowards of us all
And thus the nature here of resolution
Is sicklied o'er with the pale cast of thought,
And enterprises of great pith and moment
With this regard then currents turn awry
And lose the name of action.'

Kaufman (1971) notes that:

'Even disadvantaged members of organizations or societies ordinarily acquiesce grudgingly in the systems that treat them badly; "all experience hath shown," says the Declaration of Independence, "that mankind are more disposed to suffer, while evils are sufferable, than to right themselves by abolishing the forms to which they are accustomed".'

Thus the very essence of the situational script, particularly if it is one that has had a long run, is such as to act as a brake upon innovation, since innovation may increase rather than further reduce equivocality. In a society which values certainty and dislikes ambiguity the brake may be particularly powerful.

Competing Interpretations

Over and above this tendency to maintain the situational script simply because it is the known devil there is a likelihood that attempts to rewrite it will be resisted because the present accommodation *is* the result of competing interpretations and, by definition, is at least minimally satisfying for one or more parties involved in it. Change is likely to upset the balance of opportunities for the performance of personal scripts and, unless the social actor can be convinced that the change will benefit him or, at worst, not reduce his satisfactions, he will resist it.

Furthermore, since, according to the model, the individual has the capacity to strategically interact and to coldly consider the impact of a particular piece of behaviour, the social actor may deliberately block a proposed revision of the script even though he is aware it will not be detrimental to his interests. He may do this because of real or presumed past wrongs done to him by the actor proposing change or he may do it to establish a bargaining relationship such that he can initiate some changes in another situational script in which they are both involved.

Even if the change is forced through, as in the case of the 'new broom', or the assignment of responsibilities to a new department (as by George Brown), the competing interpretations may be such as to reduce substantially the effectiveness of the revised script and return the performance to the previous state. As Moore (1962) records:

'The new executive commonly attempts to refurbish the "old line" contacts with major diversions and other interests of central importance to the executive function. His true interest, and accessibility almost inevitably decline as he discovers that new problems preoccupy him. The aura of good feeling gradually evaporates as some new palace crowd stands between the king and his traditional subjects. Even old-timers forgetful of past cycles and disappointments, may be repeatedly trapped into believing that "this time it will be different." In detail it certainly will be the same old story with a slightly new cast of characters.' (Reproduced by persmission of Random House, Inc.)

George Brown (1972) clearly documents from his present perspective the moves made by other actors to destory the new script he devised:

'Once the heady first days had gone and the novelty had worn off, the Treasury began to reassert itself, and with its absolute mastery of the government machine gradually either filched things back or—more to the point—made it rather difficult for us to effect the grand design we had in mind so that a coherent and continuous economic policy could emerge.'

He concludes somewhat ruefully, after the Treasury has virtually reasserted control over the economy:

'So orthodox financial control won, and our basic social reformation failed. I believe the central cause of that was the failure to establish what the DEA's (Department of Economic Affairs) functions in the Government were to be. Too many people had vested interests in our department *not* succeeding. Putting it in rather crude political terms, our success meant a tremendous threat to half a dozen old-established departments. Not only the Treasury, but also Labour, the Board of Trade, Local Government, and the Scottish and Welsh Departments felt themselves threatened.' (Reproduced by permission of Victor Gollancz Ltd and St. Martin's Press.)

Thus the inherent conservatism of situational scripts and the incidence of competing interpretations of them, together with the social actor's capacity to consider his behaviour and to oppose or destroy that with which he is not in accord, weighs heavily against change. An even stronger barrier, however, is raised by the possibility that competing interpretation will not arise. Parts will be scripted, cast, and directed so as to substantially reduce the possibility of divergence.

The Casting and Direction of the Actors

As I have argued earlier elsewhere in the book each social actor comes to an encounter equipped to play certain parts and, in many circumstances, with a general awareness of the situational script that will be performed. He is aware of the regularities of social life and has been educated, socialized, and indoctrinated into the appropriate parts.

In specific settings such as those within organizations, the appropriate script will have been evolved over a number of years and may (as was the case with Schmidt) specify in great detail what part is to be performed and how it is to be performed. More importantly, for the present argument, people who wish to take part in this particular situational drama will not simply stumble into it willy-nilly; they will be selected for it.

Actors are screened and trained for the parts that they will play, more particularly if the parts offer some opportunity for improvisation or strategic interaction. Potential members are screened not only for their aptitudes but also for their attitudes and general personality traits: however skilled, he who is dubbed 'a troublemaker' is less likely to be employed than is his more docile colleague.

Once having been cast for the part, the social actor is carefully coached so that he plays his part in accordance with the wishes of those who selected him.

Thus the actor who conforms, who allows himself to be shaped in accordance with the wishes of the more powerful actors around him, may be rewarded by the offer of parts within other, more valued, situational scripts. Such promotion to star status signals to all others involved what the desirable attributes are and serves to reinforce the shaping going on throughout the enterprise. Thus many of the key actors assimilate en route through the organization the deeply-held scripts which hold it together in its present form. To quote Kaufman (1971):

'And the job itself gradually becomes a way of life for many organization members. They learn the manual, master the methods, and forge understandings with the fellows until the whole system becomes second nature to them. Directives, orders, commands, instructions, inspections, auditors' reports, and all other means of organizational control, however irksome they may once have been, are gradually accepted as one's own premises of thought and action, until compliance with them is no longer reluctant, or even indifferent, obedience but an expression of personal preference and will.' (Reproduced by permission of the University of Alabama Press.)

In my terms the social actor has become totally attached to his part and to the situational script which encompasses it. In such circumstances the script has an unchallengeable inevitability about it; there is simply no other way of performing. What is *is* because it is natural, good, and proper. It is so taken for granted, so completely internalized by the actors involved, that the question of change is not illegitimate; it is inconceivable.

Thus the dramaturgical perspective may be utilized to further the understanding of the dynamics of persistence *and* change. Change is made possible and arises out of the clash of ideas, the competing interpretations and actions actors bring to particular scenes, and is equally made less likely by these competing interpretations and actions and by the processes of selection and coaching which occur to fit the actors to the script.

Summary

In this chapter I have sought to illustrate the utility of a dramaturgical analysis of social relations. Instead of explaining behaviour as being the product of the interplay between variables or, in some fuzzy way, as due to the impact of the environment, it shows how performances are related to situational scripts and to the interpretations actors put upon the circumstances with which they are confronted. Thus it is able to account for differences in performance when actors are confronted with what appears to be 'identical' circumstances (similar technology, similar environment, etc.). It is able to accommodate notions of power—the ability to impose interpretations upon others, to develop scripts for them, and closely to monitor their performances—and can account for notions of differential attachments to particular situational scripts. Above all, by recourse to the idea that performances are constructed and sustained by a process of interpretation which, in turn, is influenced by extra organizational scripts *and* the actors experience of scripts within the organization, the perspective is able to deal with change as something which arises from interaction.

PART III

Interventions

'The activities of a playwright offer a better mode for a social scientist to follow than does the work of physicists. At least a playwright has the authenticity of his recreation of social reality checked every night in the theatre by a multitude of people. Intuitively he has a profound knowledge of the principles of social behaviour.' (Harré, 1974)

Chapter 7

The Interventionist as Critic

In this part of the book I will be concerned with the implications of the dramaturgical perspective for the practice of organization development or as I prefer to call it, following Argyris (1970), *intervention*, the process of coming 'between or among persons, groups or objects for the purpose of helping them'. While there remain substantial differences among interventionists about what constitutes sound practice there is, I believe, widespread agreement that whatever the practice it has two interrelated aspects: the generation of information and the taking of action based upon that information. In this chapter I will be concerned with the former, the analytical or diagnostic activities of the interventionist, and in the next chapter I will deal with his part in taking action. In both chapters I will seek to bring the work of others within my framework before presenting two examples of my own practice in Chapters 9 and 10.

At the base of any intervention activity and logically prior to the issue of 'What do you do about it?' is the question of 'What information do you gather and how do you order it?'. Argyris (1970) comes to this conclusion in fine rhetorical style:

'Are there any basic or necessary processes that must be fulfilled regardless of the substantive issues involved, if intervention activity is to be helpful with any line of client (individual, group, or organizational)? One contention that seems so basic as to be defined axiomatic is the generation of *valid information*. Without valid information, it would be difficult for the client to learn and for the interventionist to help.' (Reproduced by permission of Addison-Wesley Publishing Company.)

French and Bell (1973) are equally clear about the importance of diagnosis:

'OD is at heart an action programme based on valid information about the *status quo*, current problems and opportunities, and effects of actions as they relate to goal achievement. An OD programme thus starts with diagnosis and continuously employs data collecting and data analysing throughout. The requirement for diagnostic activities—activities designed to provide an accurate account of things as they really are—stems from two needs: the first need is to know the state of things, or "what is"; the second need is to know the effects or consequences of actions.' (Wendell L. French and Cecil H. Bell Jr., *Organization Development: Behavioral Science Interventions for Organization Improvement*, © 1973. By permission of Prentice-Hall, Inc., Englewood Cliffs.)

Diagnosis, however, is not an activity that takes place independent of any framework; whatever the appearances to the contrary, consultants rarely enter organizations firing off questions at random and casting around haphazardly for items of information which may be of help to them. Each and every diagnosis or analysis is based upon some more or less explicit framework of ideas. Levinson (1972) is explicit about the fact that his approach is based upon the notion that 'an organization as a whole is a system of interrelated sub-systems. In its turn, it is also a component of larger systems. . . . It affects and is affected by other systems.' His prescription for diagnosis is informed by the reification of 'organization' spelled out above:

'A comprehensive method of studying and assessing organizations for the purpose of ascertaining their points and modes of dysfunction should cover a number of major areas. It should include an evaluation of the other systems with which it interacts. It should be an ordered, systematic gathering of data as a basis for intervention or organizational change efforts. . . .

Such a method, then, should require a student of organizations to fully describe an organization's concept, objectives, plans, its view of itself as well as its relationships with others, and its leadership. It must enable the consultant to understand systems of communications, coordination, guidance, control and support. It must help him to delineate relevant environments and behaviour settings. It must be a guide to unfolding the rationale of the organization, explaining its activities, and critically evaluating the organization's adaptive adequacy, followed by a reasoned series of recommendations.'

Beckhard (1969) also adopts a systems perspective, but includes a further dimension, that of process, which may lead to different questions to those put in the Levinson tradition:

'The development of a strategy for systematic improvement of an organization demands an examination of the present state of things. Such an analysis usually looks at two broad areas. One is a diagnosis of the various subsystems that make up the total organization. These subsystems may be "natural" such as top management, the production department, or a research group; or they may be levels such as top management, middle management, or the work force.

The second area of diagnosis is the organization processes that are occurring. These include decision-making processes, communication patterns and styles, relationships between interfacing groups, the management of conflict, the setting of goals and planning methods.' (Reproduced by permission of Addison-Wesley Publishing Company.)

If the interventionist believes, as Argyris (1970) for example does, that certain kinds of behaviour contribute to system competence, then diagnosis will focus upon the presence of such kinds of behaviour:

'In short, the more individuals in systems are able to behave in an open and experimenting manner, the more they are able to express their feelings related to the substantial issues, the more they are able to help others do the same, and the higher the probability is that the system in which they work will manifest competent problem solving, decision making, and implementation of behaviour.' (Reproduced by permission of Addison-Wesley Publishing Company.)

The interventionist who works from an interactionist perspective is, of course, no exception to the general rule, and his questions and his diagnosis will be shaped by the framework of ideas with which he locates himself (or is located by other analysts). It is not that his questions need be of a substantially different kind, nor that the targets of his attention are necessarily different. Most interventionists, whatever their orientation, are interested in such things as attitudes, openness, climate, norms, patterns of decision making, goal setting, etc. The difference may lie in the ordering of the information they ferret out—the systems man will fit it into his framework, the humanist into his, the interactionist into his, and so on.

In some cases, however, the questions *are* different: that which is attended to is peculiar to the particular framework which generates the attention. The dramaturgical perspective holds that organization is not a thing standing apart from its members, but is constituted solely from the activities of the members as they engage in the process of interpreting and performing their parts in a whole array of interconnected situational scripts. In this respect it is, if not singular, certainly unusual:

'Most theories of organization grossly oversimplify the notion of the reality with which they deal. The desire to see the organization as a single kind of unit with a life of its own apart from the perceptions and beliefs of those involved in it blinds us to its complexity and the variety of organization people create around themselves. It leads us to believe that we must change some abstract thing called the 'organization' rather than socially maintained beliefs about how people should relate to one another and how they maintain desired goals. The more closely we look at organizations, the more likely we are to find expressions of diverse human meanings.' (Reproduced by special persmission from *The Journal of Applied Behavioral Science*. 'Organizations as social inventions: rethinking assumptions about change', by T. Barr Greenfield, Volume 9, No. 5, p. 571. Copyright 1973 NTL Institute for Applied Behavioral Science.)

Thus diagnosis from such a perspective would be concerned, among other things, with the meanings that social actors bring to and derive from their interlocked behaviours.

All of this is by way of a lengthy preamble to the spelling out of what analysis or diagnosis may look like from a dramaturgical perspective. It is not to claim that it is in all respects better than diagnosis based upon any other framework, but merely to state that it is different and does draw attention to features of life in organizations likely to be ignored by other approaches.

From the dramaturgical perspective (and neatly contained within it), analysis may be seen as the process of criticism, the act of estimating the qualities and character of an event or set of relationships and of passing judgement (especially though not necessarily unfavourably) upon it. The dramatic critic is concerned with such issues as the dramatic personae, the setting, the text, or script and the realization of these characteristics in performance. The critic or analyst of social dramas is equally disposed to talk of actors, scripts, purposes, and performances.

A dramaturgically informed analysis of relations within an organization could be concerned with the following issues:

(1) What are the situational scripts, 'the boring little stories' that constitute this particular organization? How did these scripts arise?

(2) Are the situational scripts marked by a relatively high incidence of strategic interaction or are they relatively closely scripted and directed?

(3) Who are the social actors involved? What interpretations do they bring to and derive from their interactions? What ends are they pursuing in their association with particular scripts?

(4) Whose interpretations, performances, and ends create and sustain the situational scripts? Has the script the quality of imposition, if so by whom, or is it the expression of a consensually improvised mutual accommodation?

(5) How do particular actors play their parts? What strategies do they adopt (if any)? How are they selected for and trained for these parts?

(6) How attached to their parts are particular individuals in particular situational scripts?

(7) How aware are the social actors of their present scripts and performances and of alternative scripts and alternative performances?

(8) What pressures are there to change scripts and performances, from whence do they emanate, how strong are they, and what is the perceived likelihood of scripts being changed?

Such an analysis is very difficult to undertake at a distance or by means of questionnaires and structured interviews. It required that the analyst or critic be deeply familiar with his material; dramatic criticism of this kind demands that the critic attends the theatre in person and does not rely upon the text alone or upon the opinions of others gathered at one remove from his subject matter. The required approach is to see 'the acting unit as confronted with an operating situation that it has to handle and vis-a-vis which it has to work out a line of action' (Blumer, 1969). The appropriate critical stance consists in seeking to understand what the situations look like from the point of view of the participants. It is impossible to become completely identified with the perspective of particular social actors, but it is possible to seek to understand what features the actor takes into account in forming his action and, by interview and observation, to make some preliminary assessment of the nature of his predispositions and the likelihood that he will seek to perform certain parts rather than others. Only by close attention, by a deep immersion in his material, can the observer hope to apprehend the nature of particular situational scripts and their associated 'whiffs'. Each elaboration of the script and each movement in the temporary (or relatively permanent) accommodation is temporally linked with the previous accommodation. Failure to observe closely over time means that one shuts a major door to the understanding of any particular situational script. Equally, it is only through the process of close and lengthy association with particular actors that one is able to determine the strength of their attachments to particular parts and scripts. It is not enough simply to ask them (though it may be necessary to do so); there is no substitute for the observation of how people actually perform as they go about their daily work.

The character of the dramaturgical analysis can best be understood when it is related to the analysis of a particular organization. It would be comparatively easy at this juncture to provide one of my own studies as a base on which the dramaturgical model could be erected, but it is probably more powerful if I use material not written with this perspective in mind—material that, while not shaped by my analysis, is explicable in terms of it. I have chosen for the purpose Argyris' (1974) book *Behind the Front Page* and his description of events and the theoretical apparatus he uses to analyse them will be compared with the elements of dramaturgical analysis I have suggested in the previous pages.

Behind the Front Page

The richly detailed study presented by Argyris is concerned with the activities of the top executives of *The Daily Planet* and covers a period of three years. My recasting of his material deals only with the 'diagnostic phase', lasting approximately one year, during which time Argyris observed behaviour and interviewed the leading performers. His method was 'to observe in person actual task-oriented encounters and meetings.' Most of the meetings he recorded. The data then obtained were analysed in line with his own theoretical ideas (derived from earlier studies) and yielded valuable information on the interstructured behaviour at the heart of the organization:

'The results of my scoring procedure tell us about the way people actually behave in meetings. They do not tell us how the same persons felt, nor how they might behave if they were observed under different conditions. These results address themselves to the behaviour that creates the living system, and not to the individual personalities of the executives.'

This is a reasonable approximation, that is, to what I have termed a situational script.

The particular situational script which occupies much of Argyris' analysis is that of the news meeting, the purpose of which was 'of getting a more effective intellectual shaping of the newspaper'. Whatever the content of these meetings, Argyris (and some of the participants) found them to be predictable. The news meeting, and most other meetings for that matter, tended to be settings in which

(1) Opinions were expressed: 'The most frequently observed behaviour was people owning up to or describing their points of view; the group meetings were full of articulate people telling others their respective points of view.'

(2) Ideas were sought from the superior 'trying to find out what the superior wanted and what he was going to do'.

(3) Competition was the norm: 'Behaviour in group meetings tended to be competitive.'

(4) Win–lose dynamics was the pattern. Participants 'spoke just to hear themselves speak' and to 'impress their boss'.

(5) Evaluation and control were to the forefront of interaction: 'I don't see

what's new about that!', 'This is a terrific story! Very important. We ought to! (defines what ought to be done).'

(6) Expression of feelings was not evident: 'The least frequently observed behaviour—indeed, it was not reported even once—was a person expressing his own feelings or being open to other people's feelings.'

(7) Risk taking with ideas or feelings was low: 'If one learns to be careful not to rock the boat, then one learns to think twice about taking risks.'

(8) No helping behaviour was displayed. 'The scores for *not* helping others, on the other hand, were some of the highest that I have ever recorded in all my studies. These scenes indicate that persons were cutting each other off in order to seize scarce "air time" in any meeting.'

(9) Little listening to others occurred. Since members of groups meetings focused most of their energies on 'gaining air time, being persuasive, and winning, there tended to be very little listening to other's views'.

Argyris captures the flavour of the news meeting in the following passage in which, in effect, he provides a critical analysis of the situational script:

'The competitive, win-lose dynamics tended to encourage modes of "selling". "Selling" tended to make the speaker feel that he was being articulate and intellectually powerful. However, this very power could act to reduce the probabilities that the "customer" would buy. The customer might sense that the speaker's power was more emotional than rational, yet notice that the speaker was insisting he was being rational and was asking others to be the same (let's look at the facts). The listener could then mistrust the "sales pitch". He could decide that the speaker was mainly trying to win him over to protect his own departmental interests, not trying to help create a climate where the best solutions could be found or a new idea could be created.

Under these conditions, participants at meetings tended to immunize themselves against infection by the enthusiasm of the seller. They would try to deflate him or cut off his speech; or time him out and then silently begin to prepare their own sales pitches; or listen only to find weaknesses in his expressed position. Upon perceiving any of these reactions, the original seller would feel less effective. He would react by selling harder and by evaluating the others as somewhat stubborn for defending a "narrow departmental or personal view".

Thus there was a recycling which tended to increase the selling and competitiveness. This made individuals feel they were rarely heard or understood, which in turn led them to be very careful and articulate in verbalizing their thoughts. They concentrated more on preparing their contribution than on listening to others. Moreover, once they began speaking they continued until all the accumulated ideas had been heard. One result was that the time available to be "on the air" was scarce.' (Reproduced by permission of Jossey-Bass Ltd., London and San Francisco.)

The script and the processes of interpretation, self-presentation, and altercast-ing, which sustain it as outlined in the passage quoted, leave little apparent room for strategic interaction. Opinion giving was the norm but '. . . although people spoke their minds, they did so, especially when there was a discussion of important issues, in a way which reinforced conformity. . . .' The script demanded that the social actors perform as if they were open and confronting, but not too open nor too confronting. Thus 'subordinates learned to be "controlled rebels", to deviate carefully, and if they were to deviate to do it effectively and rarely'. For example: 'There is a lifestyle of being a renegade. Not a renegade; a controlled rebel. To know how far you can push. I think this is something everybody looks upon as good. It isn't being the "yes man" but a kind of "yes man" who argues here and gives there.'·

The situational script was clearly one that induced people to conform to the pattern of opinion giving; attempts to produce other performances were resisted. Argyris notes that he was not able to "observe a single instance in which a group member openly expressed an issue that was ambiguous to him and perhaps others'.When such opportunities were advanced by superiors, subordinates 'seemed to interpret the invitation for exploration and thinking out loud as an opportunity to speak and shine'.

Argyris' social actors, the top forty men in the business, brought to and derived from the news meetings some interpretations which, in turn, affected their performances within the meetings. Many of them, for example, considered that meetings were a 'big waste of time', that competition was a desirable attribute in a newspaper man, that win–lose dynamics were a necessary part of the game and were 'fun', that conflict should be handled 'diplomatically' or covertly, and that threatening information should be withheld. Most of them believed that 'effective leadership is strong, directive, believes in competitiveness, and confronts interpersonal conflicts covertly'.

Given these interpretations it is hardly surprising that many of the social actors adopted a stance of 'over-respect' towards their superiors. 'The individual represents to them an individual who has won, and who, because of his power, can continue to win.' The result is that the situational script for the news meeting tends to be imposed, however gently and with a large degree of acceptance on the part of the others, by the chairman. The other social actors may see it as a waste of time and an ineffective forum for the resolution of issues, but they will go along with the chairman's wish to have everyone participate even when they recognize that he 'does dominate it, but not in a harsh way. From the very beginning he opens it up with his ideas and he has ten ideas for every one that everybody else has.' Thus the situational script is created by the chairman who wants the news meeting to provide opportunities for everyone to participate in the generation of 'new ideas' and the exploration of 'long range planning'. It is sustained by the other social actors accepting his predisposition to dominate and by themselves playing the roles of 'controlled rebels'.

The actors are cast for their parts and trained through a lengthy process. Many of their interpretations of what constitutes appropriate performance are derived from generalized scripts not peculiar to the organizations. Argyris notes, for example, that people are educated, 'beginning early in life', into what constitutes 'acceptable behaviour' with regard to problem solving, decision making, and decision taking. The interpretations found within the staff of *The Daily Planet*, emphasizing fast accomplishment, competitiveness, control of others, loyalty to those with power, and avoidance of overt conflict, are interpretations which are inculcated and sustained outside the doors of *The Daily Planet* as well as within them. Within the organization social actors learn the script, learn how 'far they can go' and are carefully coached: 'They think that fascinates most about my job is teaching. Take in some kid and make him, mold him into a finished newsman.' Not that this is to be done harshly: 'I try to be gentle with them. I try to avoid being authoritarian. Of course it is up to me to show them the way to do the job. I've got to assume that the way I do it is correct.'

Some of the social actors have well-developed strategies for dealing with the news meeting, not only of the 'controlled rebel' form but ones which have been evolved to meet specific 'whiffs'. What if you want to use the competitive, win–lose situational script as 'resources for ideas without losing something'? The answer, according to one of the social actors, is 'brain-picking'—asking questions in order to clarify one's own thoughts, but asking them (because of the win–lose dynamics) without seeming to need the information. Other individuals adopted different strategies, some preferring to remain silent and withdrawn: 'I find the best way to disagree is to remain quiet and deal with the issue outside the group meeting.'

Such comments, of course, reflect a high degree of awareness of what is going on but, as is so often the case, what is going on, be it a waste of time or an opportunity to perform, is created and sustained by *others* not by me. Argyris notes that in many of the interviews there was 'an implicit assumption that it is the *other* person who comes to talk and to impress or who is not effective'. Equally strongly held is a view that there are no alternatives (other than to cancel all meetings), since that which is observable is attributable to 'human nature'. Alternatives are inconceivable and, to some extent, unwelcome. In answer to Argyris' question 'Could you conceive of a group situation where these rivalries and hurt feelings could be discussed with the men involved?', all but two of his respondents replied 'no'.

The pressure for change, such as it was, appeared to come from the chairman (though this passage is somewhat confusing in Argyris' book), who wanted the focus to move away from himself and onto the other participants: 'He wanted to act as a facilitator of discussion rather than a controller.' The other participants do not address the issue directly, but are clearly pessimistic about the possibility of *any* change, as this interchange between Argyris and an executive illustrates:

'Argyris: So in a sense, it stems from the facts that each of these men has his own goals and own interests?
Executive: Exactly.
Argyris: I infer from your comments that you don't think there's much anyone can do about that. It's human nature. Is that correct?
Executive: Exactly.'
(Reproduced by permission of Jossey Bass Ltd., London and San Francisco.)

In summary, Argyris' analysis depicts a situational script in which, whatever its original purposes, social actors compete for attention and seek to achieve their own individual purposes at the expense of others—a situation which is sustained by the training of the social actors, by their inability to conceive of alternatives, and by a deep pessimism about the possibility of change.

The interventionist as critic, however, is not content merely to analyse the situational scripts in the manner outlined above. As critic he simultaneously reviews the activities of the players and makes some evaluation of the drama he sees unfolding before him. His mind is not a *tabula rasa* on which impressions may be written; like all social actors he comes to the situational script of criticism equipped with some taken-for-granted views and a predisposition to play a certain kind of role.

He reviews what he sees going on against a model he holds in his mind, informed by theory and experience, of what constitutes sound performance. He may be obsessed with ideas about exploitation or self-actualization, or about the importance of providing opportunity for extempore performance or the exercise of discretion. He may be convinced that the expression of emotions is vital to smooth performance. He may think parts should be equally distributed and that no one actor should constantly be at the centre of the stage. He may, like any other actor, have a whole array of interpretations.

The interventionist as critic does not simply soak up that with which he is confronted; he *attends* to some issues and ignores others. If he is an organization development man he will tend to arrive at the social theatre with ideas of good performances being marked by the opportunities it provides the actors for collaboration, growth, discretion, authenticity, the expression of feeling, utilization of their whole personality, etc., and he will rate what he sees accordingly along some or all of these dimensions.

Argyris (1974) makes *his* diagnosis and effects *his* criticism against a background of experience and ideas which lead him to believe that performance is enhanced when feelings are not excluded from expression, discussion, and consideration. Not surprisingly, therefore, his analyses, among other things, are concerned with the expression of feelings displayed in the particular situational script. His analysis is in no way 'objective'; he, like us all, has a script to follow.

The interventionist functions primarily as a critic and is hired as such; his analysis is not neutral and nor, as I shall demonstrate, are his suggestions for action.

Chapter **8**

The Interventionist as Dramaturg

Now that I have offered some ideas as to the kind of information gathered and as to the manner in which it is analysed by the interventionist as critic I wish to turn to the activities of the interventionist as dramaturg. Willet (1964) informs us that a dramaturg is 'a permanent play-reader, playwright and literary odd-job man who is part of every German theatre'. Among other things he is employed as a rewrite man and assistant director; he may be called upon to doctor plays, to add, delete or rewrite lines, parts, scenes, and, very occasionally, entire scripts. No self-respecting theatre is complete without at least one dramaturg. What I am proposing is that every self-respecting organization should have its dramaturg, employed to tinker with and, occasionally, to help in the transformation of entire situational scripts. For the purposes of this exposition I take such 'literary odd-jobs' to be the function of the consultant, be he internal or external, and it is this facet of his activities that I now wish to consider.

I have proposed in an earlier chapter that change in social relationships or in attachment to particular parts is of two forms: that which is the product of almost continuous adjustment and accommodation which proceeds in a stepped sequence and that which I have termed *discontinuous change*, often associated with crisis and always involving a radical departure from that which has preceded it. The interventionist as critic and dramaturg may be involved in both forms.

The interventionist working within the first tradition which, for the sake of labelling, I will term *gradualism*, can bring about change by helping the social actor (or actors) play parts better. In helping the actor play his part better, with sharper definition and greater skill, he is not acting as a rewrite man, but as a coach and a counsellor. He is not seeking to change anybody's lines or anybody's relationships directly, but is attempting to bring about a better fit between the actor and the part he is required to play. Hunt (1974) notes that there is a potential conflict between the needs of the individual and the demands of the script when he writes that

'the currency of counselling has two sides: what a worker wants from his job and his life and what the organization wants of the worker. On the one hand in varying measure, workers want such things as a steady, decent job, satisfying relations with fellow workers and supervisors, a sense of belonging and identity, recognition and equitable compensation, freedom from exploitation, and a chance to express and develop skills, just to name some of the possibilities. The organization, on the other hand, expects the worker to work hard, to meet standards efficiently, to observe rules of conduct on (and perhaps off) the job, to be willing to see management's side of things, to be responsible and mature, to be cooperative, and, above all, to be loyal.' (Reproduced by permission of Wadsworth Publishing Company, Inc.)

There can be little doubt that much, if not all, of the counselling which takes place within organizations is carried out without any questioning of the script; efficiency, productivity, responsibility, cooperation, maturity, and loyalty are to be expected and counselling consists of helping the actor play his part better in achieving these ends without detracting too much from his own needs.

The goals of coaching as of counselling, again spelled out by Hunt (1974), are:

'1. To reduce loads of anxiety prevalent in work environments and to accomplish increased comfort and morale on the parts of organization members.
2. To increase the self-respect and self-confidence of organization members.
3. To lower the degrees of defensiveness among organization members, thereby helping to open channels of communication.
4. To enhance the system's overall problem-solving and enhance its effectiveness and productivity.' (Reproduced by permission of Wadsworth Publishing Company, Inc.)

Thus the interventionist working from a gradualistic perspective is likely to be concerned, for example, with helping a social actor (or social actors) run meetings better by coaching him (or them) in such skills as listening, encouraging others to speak, clarifying, summarizing, and so on. He will not be suggesting different casts for the meeting script, nor will he be indulging in a wholesale rewrite of it, but will be seeking to have it better performed. Changes in the cast and scripts may arise out of this activity, but such are not his primary concern as a counsellor (or dramatic coach).

The distinction I want to make is well illustrated in this final extract from Hunt (1974):

'Imagine a clerical employee whose technical performance is altogether satisfactory and who has expressed supervisory aspirations. He has recently grown a beard, which he maintains in a meticulous state of repair. His immediate superior, however has reason to think that the employee's beard is prejudicial to his future in the organization because of the attitudes of certain members of the review panel responsible for selecting management trainees.

This is actually a familiar kind of case. The question is whether it is part of the supervisor's responsibility to counsel the employee about the matter of his personal appearance. It would seem that the answer should be an equivocal yes. It is equivocal because any manager is wise to have some trepidation about these personal involvements and about overextending the bonds of organizational interest. In this area, a conservative posture seems desirable. Yet, in an employee-centred framework, the supervisor has a re-sponsibility to *the* subordinate that is not served by silence. Furthermore, assuming it to be one of the supervisor's normal functions to participate in management development, his active responsibility as an agent of the organization is plain.' (Reproduced by permission of Wadsworth Publishing Company, Inc.)

The example is trivial, but the distinction it embodies is not. The concern of the counsellor is in fitting the employee to the script, advising him that beards are unacceptable, and not in seeking to bring about a change in the scripts such that the issue of beards is considered openly. Much of counselling and, I shall argue later, much of organization development, is of the nature of dramatic coaching, fitting the actor to his part and accepting that the broad lines of the script are appropriate and to be taken for granted. It does not follow, of course, that this is necessarily manipulative; in many cases the actor seeks out the dramatic coach and signs up, as it were, for lessons in elocution and fencing. In most cases the act of coaching is collaborative and neither party questions the fundamental script nor the allocation of roles. In some cases, however, coaching involves the questioning of the fundamental scripts and the allocation of parts. It is not inconceivable that the approach might be used to, say, enlarge and enhance the negotiating skills of labour union leaders or to teach minority groups how to better deploy their resources and achieve their aims. Coaching in practice may tend to be somewhat conservative, but there is no reason why this should necessarily be the case. In one situation with which I was associated a senior executive called me in to talk about the new position that had been offered him. As we talked about what was expected of him it became clear to us both that all was not well with his relationship with his superior who had assigned him to these new duties. Not only was the new position attended by all kinds of difficulties, the possibility of even raising these difficulties with his superior was made almost impossible by the obstacles the latter was seen to put in the way of such an interaction. Having redefined the issue as not being the impossibility of the task but the impossibility of talking about the task to the managing director, together we developed and carefully rehearsed a strategy for bringing about the desired discussion. Thus a coaching relationship was used, and may be used, to effect change in relationships as well, as is more usually the case—to fit 'square pegs into round holes'.

Dramatic coaching represents an approach to change which operates within the script and, in many cases, without there being any awareness that the script (if it is recognized as such) can be questioned or adapted. It is probably helpful at this point to introduce a distinction drawn by Watzlowick, Weakland, and Fisch (1974) between first-order and second-order change.

They argue that there are 'two different types of change, one that occurs within a given system which itself remains unchanged, and one where occurrence changes and system itself'. Watzlowick, Weakland, and Fisch go on to give a real example of the distinction which, happily, accords with the position I wish to develop:

'To exemplify this distinction in more behavioural terms: a person having a nightmare can do many things *in* his dream—run, hide, fight, scream, jump off a cliff etc.—but no change from any one of these behaviours to another would ever terminate the nightmare. *We shall henceforth refer to this kind of change as first-order change.* The one way *out of* a dream involves a change from dreaming to waking. Waking, obviously is no longer a part of the dream, but a change to an altogether different state. This kind of change will be referred to as *second-order change.*' (Reproduced by permission of W. W. Norton & Company, Inc.)

Recasting this distinction in my terms, I would argue that some changes occur within the script as part of the process of mutual accommodation and that these changes occur without any awareness on the part of the actors that they are operating within a situational script. Such changes are of a continuous, first-order nature. Second-order change occurs when the actor becomes or is made aware of the nature of the situational scripts within which he normally takes his part. Second-order change involves the social actors taking a *metatheatrical* perspective on their actions and implies, by this very feature, that change of this order is of a discontinuous nature.

Awareness is the key to second-order change. As Berger (1963) puts it: ' . . . all revolutions begin in transformations of consciousness'. Once the social actor becomes aware of his part, becomes sufficiently detached from it so as not to play it without thought and reflection, he sees the possibility of changing the way he performs. The notion of role-distance outlined earlier in this book is useful in this context since the actor who is distanced from his role *is* aware of the nature of the role into which he is cast; he may not be able for reasons of power or skill to do anything about it or, even given the power and the skill, he may not wish to do anything about it, but he is aware of his part and some aspects of the script.

Thus the art of the interventionist lies in capitalizing upon the amount of role-distance there is already in the system, in increasing the amount of role distance, and in creating opportunities for as many actors as possible to take a metatheatrical perspective on their activities. From such a perspective the actors become aware of their own theatricality, the nature of the parts they play, and the scripts they create, sustain, and can transform.

Taking a metatheatrical perspective is an act of alienation, a large-scale effort at role-distance. Alienation, in the way that I am using the term, is the art of making the familiar strange by stepping outside it. It is the process of disrupting the taken-for-grantedness of everyday life. As Brecht (1940) puts it: 'We make something natural incomprehensible in a certain way, but only in order to make it more comprehensible afterwards. In order for something known to become perceived it must cease to be ordinary; one must break with the habitual notion that the thing in question requires no elucidation.' He notes that 'a thing that has not been changed for a long time appears unchangeable', which leads Holthusen (1961) to declare that 'it can be changed as soon as it has been frightened out of its naturalness by alienation'. Putting the frighteners on situational scripts is at the centre of organization development, certainly as I practise it. The creation of role-distance and alienation, the achievement of a metatheatrical perspective, creates circumstances such that '*giveness* becomes *possibility*'. Picasso (Daix, 1965) points to a very similar function when discussing his work:

'When I paint, I always try to give an image people are not expecting, and, beyond that, one they reject. That's what interests me. It's in this sense that I mean I always try to be subversive. That is, I give a man an image of himself whose elements are collected from among the usual ways of seeing things in traditional painting and then reassembled in a fashion that is unexpected and disturbing enough to make it impossible for him to escape the questions it raises.'

The potential for second-order change, of course, is an intrinsic part of the dramaturgical perspective. As outlined in the previous chapters each and every actor has the capacity to stand aside from the interaction to which he is party, to consider it, and to develop strategies to realize his own ends. In most circumstances given the *naturalness* of them he is unlikely to utilize this capacity, but it is there nevertheless. We can construct and reconstruct the daily drama of everyday life in our heads, we can and do evaluate and appraise performances, and we can and do (very occasionally) consider the theatrical nature of our interactions. Thus what I am suggesting, the adoption of a metatheatrical stance, is not in and of itself alien to the nature of man as I have depicted it. Indeed it is a basic if underutilized capacity which the interventionist can energize if he so wishes.

The Drama of Feedback

The usual way for the interventionist to make use of this capacity is for him to feed back to the social actors concerned his analysis of what he has learned from observing and talking to them. He then provides them with and, hopefully, involves them in a critical review of their activities. Argyris (1974), for example, followed up his analysis (which I somewhat impertinently recast into my framework in the last chapter) with a feedback session in which he sought to have 'the participants feel some sense of concern about their own effectiveness and the organization's effectiveness. Thus the first use of the diagnosis is to see whether the members will confirm it, and if they do, whether they will respond by asking for help to overcome the problem.' Feedback, in one form or another, is a central feature of attempts to bring about second-order change. As Golembiewski (1972) makes clear, it is the classic approach:

'In the typical case an Organization Development consultant interviews a manager and his immediate subordinates, or he might use a questionnaire or some instrument to gather the needed data. Then the consultant reports his summary findings and observations to all those interviewed in a total session. The goal is to facilitate public coping of the "Now that the consultant mentions it" variety. . . .'

In effect the interventionist as critic is saying, 'Here are the scripts you are involved in as I see them. The first question is do you recognize this as a picture of where you are? If so, is it where you want to be?'

Feedback sessions reveal the interventionist as a rewrite man. All the principal actors are assembled in an appropriate setting (usually away from the hurly-burly of their everyday scripts) and are invited to listen and to join in the critical review of the activities which is about to unfold before them. Whatever form the feedback may take (numerical, pictorial, or verbal) the interventionist seeks to have the actors recognize the activities to which he draws attention and, if possible, seeks to have them build upon this recognition. Here is Argyris (1972) again (for some obscure reason choosing to identify himself as X):

'X: I'd like to point out a dilemma. During the Interviews, many of you expressed hopes that P would change some of his behaviour. He was described as a person who, in many cases unrealisingly, rejected people, lashed out, hurt them, and so on. Is the group backing off just as it is getting at one of the critical issues? Am I making a mountain out of a molehill? . . .

E: What you are seeing is the normal expectation of men in their forties and fifties faced with having to be honest with each other and quite rightly being unable to do it.

G: When I hear P's faults being described, I realize a lot of them apply to me. I feel somewhat guilty. I too have the same problems. Possibly this is true of many of us.

P: But we must discuss these issues. As all of you know, there is an issue that we planned to discuss here which has been on and off for four years. Each of you tell me your views and then you leave and nothing happens.

H: After four years of waiting I think P should make the decision.

D: But how can he? He doesn't really know where we stand.

P: I guess I can make assumptions.

A: Yes, but your assumptions have been wrong.

X: Perhaps you can test your assumptions.

C: Why do we have to focus on P? Why can't we talk about the best decision-making structure? Why do we have to get into this behavioural science crap, if you'll forgive the expression.

P: But will we learn anything?

E: How can we talk about this in the abstract? He is the only P we have.

G: I'm sympathetic. This conversation is focusing increasingly on you as an individual.

P: I want it to.

A: He's asking for it.

P: I want to listen, learn, and come back at you. (*Laughter*)

X: Perhaps this is another fear. If we talk about P, then it makes it more legitimate for him and others to talk about us.

B: Does it make sense to analyze motives? I think we ought to stop this.

X: I agree with you that analyzing motives may be ineffective. However, if my diagnosis is correct, the people in this room—indeed in the entire organization—spend much of their time analyzing motives, never testing their analyses and then acting on them.

P: Why is it necessary to look at how we operate as a group? Let's take an issue and discuss it.

X: Once in a while it's important to open up the hood of your car and see if the motor is working effectively.

D: The old P used to say that if you had a car going 50 miles an hour, never open up the hood.

X: This is a choice that we now have to make. So we want to look at our behaviour?

P: I think we have to. We can't go back to the old days. I doubt if that will work. You and others ask for involvement. I am trying to give it. My difficulty is that I try to involve everyone and I get no decision made.'

(Reproduced by permission of Jossey-Bass Ltd., London and San Francisco.)

The language employed by the interventionist as dramaturg may not be that of the theatre, it may be that of the system theorist or humanist, but his objective is to bring about circumstances in which the social actors no longer unconsciously or defensively simply *respond* to situational scripts but rather become sufficiently aware of them to perceive (if not to actually *construct*) alternatives.

I have deliberately reintroduced the word 'dramaturg' to emphasize that the interventionist is not a neutral figure in this process. As I have shown in my discussion of his behaviour as critic, he has values and ideas which colour his perception and influence his actions. He may be more aware of these values and ideas and he may have more skill in deploying them strategically rather than simply blindly following them wherever they may lead him, but he is not an intellectual eunuch and, since he is not, he is interested in the new scripts which may arise from the interaction having certain qualities lacking in the old ones. Again Argyris (1974) is representative in his own values if somewhat clearer than most about his activities as dramaturg:

'R: Would you prefer it the other way (go into a training group)?
X: It's difficult for me to answer that question. But my inference, after experiencing the degree of genuine resistance here, is that this group would be more comfortable working on key organizational problems first and then examining interpersonal relationships. *I'm willing to go along if I can be free to bring up the interpersonal issues when they seem important to me.* You can, of course, stop discussions of this kind at any time. But if you stop too many of them, then I'll have to say that I can't be of much help. (Italics mine)
B: I have a little trouble with this. First of all, I've felt from the beginning, when you came here, you were arguing for openness.
X: Yes.
B: Arguing for men to say honestly what they felt.
X: Yes, but in such a way that others would also be honest about how they felt.'
(reproduced by permission of Jossey-Bass Ltd., London and San Francisco.)

Argyris (1974) is clearly pushing for the new scripts to be marked by openness, honesty, and trust and is seen to be so doing by the other social actors. His stance may be collaborative, his approach to the rewriting based upon research and logic, but it is the approach of someone with a script of his own and not that of a hack writer who will ghost any script required for the money.

Some Examples of the Dramaturgical Perspective of Intervention

As I have noted elsewhere in this book, the prevailing models of man are either systems oriented or derived from a humanistic base. Occasionally, though not necessarily explicitly, the dramaturgical perspective is utilized. Dayal and Thomas (1968) rely heavily upon an unacknowledged dramaturgical base in their programme of organizational development in a new company. Their work is worth outlining in some detail since it illustrates neatly the use of the model (albeit implicitly) and the stages of the process of developing and implementing new roles.

Developing a New Organization

Dayal and Thomas (1968) took it upon themselves to discover the emergent situational scripts and the degree of attachment the actors had to these scripts and, in particular, to their own parts within them. From their critical review of the scripts, Dayal and Thomas proposed that they needed to involve the actors in a renegotiation of the scripts and of their parts. The language the authors use is traditional, but their intention is clear and may readily be subsumed in the terms outlined above:

'The second task was to aim at developing interdependence among the network of roles constituting the management team. How does one role depend upon and relate with other roles? What are the mutual obligations and responsibilities? . . .'

The vehicle to be used for renegotiation was group discussion and a procedure which was eventually termed the role analysis technique (RAT). Deriving from the ideas of Kahn *et al.* (1964), the technique consists of a number of steps. The focal role (the particular part to be focused upon) initiates the discussion and declares what he takes to be the purpose of his role in the overall objectives of the company. He lists the elements of his part, the duties and activities which constitute, in his eyes, its *raison d'etre*. The rest of the actors discuss this and add or delete items as agreed to be appropriate.

The next step involves the focal role incumbent in listing what he requires of others in order to play his part effectively. These expectations are listed, discussed, modified, rejected, elaborated, and eventually consolidated. 'In the end a workable formula is evolved describing mutual expectations and obligations.'

The third step follows neatly from the second in that the other actors now declare what they want of the focal role holder in the performance of his part. Similarly, these expectations are discussed, modified, and so on.

The fourth step involves the role incumbent in writing up his part and consolidating the script which has been mutually constructed. That this is essentially theatrical may be seen from the way it is dramatized by the interventionist; the step involves

'(a) a set of activities classified as the prescribed and the discretionary elements of the role (the degree of extempore performance permissible),
(b) the obligations of the role to each role in its set, and
(c) the expectations of this role from others in its set.'

The fifth set consists of a review of the projected part before another focal role is analysed.

Thus the entire script is elaborated and agreed between actors and interventionists. That the latter in fact operated as dramaturgs may be inferred from their attempts to influence the emerging scripts by (1) providing 'reading material' derived from 'Wilfred Brown, Elliot Jacques, Douglas McGregor, Iswan Dayal, Richard Beckhard, Warren G. Bennis and others' and by (2) participating 'when certain concepts needed clarification' and 'at times raising "issues which we felt the group needed to consider" '.

Having written the drama and cast the parts it seemed only necessary to realize it on the organizational stage and to provide an opportunity for the regular assumption of a metatheatrical perspective such that the parts to be played were not performed 'mechanistically'. 'The group evolved a plan whereby individuals would hold periodic discussions on the nature of their work together.' These sessions would focus on how well performances were agreeing with 'expectations and obligations, why not, and what might be done about it'.

Dayal and Thomas (1968) add substantially to the understanding of the activities of the interventionist as dramaturg. They remind us that although awareness may be necessary to the effectance of second-order change it is by no means enough. However smart the interventionist as critic is, very little will change simply by presentation of his critical review, even if the social actors accept it as a plausible one (which is by no means an easy state to arrive at, as we shall discuss later in this chapter). The interventionist as dramaturg helps the actors to generate alternative scripts, works carefully with them to build up the parts necessary to the enactment of such scripts, coaches the individual players in the details of their parts, and provides an opportunity for the scripts to be reviewed and modified if appropriate.

The activities of the interventionist as dramaturg can be seen in some of the other examples of intervention informed by dramaturgical concepts such as role. Golembiewski (1972) creates awareness and invites the participants, literally, to write the script at one and the same time. The situational script required an actor to play a part in the drama of headquarters and field relations. The script was well established, an actor was recruited from the field, rapidly became cast (by his previous associates) as a 'headquarters' man', ran into conflict with them, lost the subsequent battle, and was removed from his part. The process usually took less than a year. Golembiewski (1972) was invited to develop a design to create a script whereby the next incumbent would 'be in office at least 18 months'. He took what he terms a 'direct approach' and suggested that the integrative executive's part should be rewritten by 'the six field managers, three of whom were candidates for the position and all of whom would be affected in one direct way or another by the outcome'.

The strength of the design is that it forces the executives concerned to take a strategic interactive perspective. It places them in a circumstance where they must 'put themselves in the role of the actor' and consider the impact of their behaviour on the joint performance. It also invites them to rewrite their own parts and that of the intergrating executive in such a manner that the script is more acceptable to each of them and, finally, it invites them to anticipate the situational 'whiffs' and resolve them 'both formally in the job description and behaviourally in moving toward the creation of norms and attitudes that could be applied . . . to the resolution of the jurisdictional issues that might develop later'.

Sherwood and Glidewell (1975) also make sense of the role idea in the paper *Planned Renegotiation: A Norm-setting OD Intervention*. They present 'a clear and simple model' of how roles are established and changed. They see relationships as cycling through (1) the sharing of information and expectations, then (2) commitment to a set of expectations which governs behaviour during a period (3) of stability and productivity, when, for the most part you do what I expect of you and I do what you expect of me, until (4) disruption occurs and the possibility of change enters the system. The authors propose that 'Where this simple model of how roles are established and how they change is available to the actors and where they have skills in sharing their reactions, feelings and perceptions about their relationship' (in my terms where a metatheatrical perspective can be achieved), 'change can be introduced in a controlled and systematic way through planned renegotiation.'

Where a particular social actor 'feels a pinch' (in my terms a loss of attachment) with regard to a particular role, he signals that he needs to talk about this and the possibility of a rewriting of the script is then raised. Thus, argue Sherwood and Glidewell, by anticipating crises roles can be renegotiated in circumstances where the actors have more control and less anxiety.

Harrison (1972) utilizes a similar procedure, but is characteristically tough-minded about the nature of it. The name of the technique—role negotiation—describes the process, which involves changing by means of negotiation with other interested parties the role which an individual or group perform in an organization:

'By an individual or group's *role* I mean the work arrangements he has with the others . . . what activities he is supposed to perform, what decisions he can make, to whom he reports and about what and how often, who can legitimately tell him what to do and under what circumstances, and so on . . . what I mean by *role* includes not only the formal job description, but also the informal understandings, agreements, expectations and arrange-ments with others which determine the way one person's or group's work affects or fits in with another.'

Changes in parts and situational scripts arise as the interventionist presses the social actors to be explicit about their parts and the part they expect to be played by others. Each social actor is encouraged to be 'open and specific about what he wants others to do *more* or do *better* or do *less* or maintain unchanged'. Again, as with the work of Sherwood and Glidewell, Harrison's model involves the actors in stepping outside their usual, taken-for-granted routines and adopting a strategic perspective on the interaction. And again it makes the assumption that insight or awareness is not enough. The interventionist working within the Harrison framework urges the social actors to write down his expectations and to pass those proposed script revisions to the other social actors involved with him in the scripts. At the same time as he passes the revised scripts to the others he also indicates (again in writing) what revisions in his script he is willing to trade for the changes he requires of others. The rewriting is then an explicit process of accommodation in which 'two or more members agree to change behaviour in exchange for some desired change on the part of the other'. The process is only complete when the revised parts are written down such that all can see what has been given up and what is expected in return.

Second-order change is thus brought about in circumstances where the social actors achieve a metatheatrical perspective on their situational scripts;—where they are able, relatively dispassionately, to observe and reflect upon their everyday actions and the consequences of such actions for each other. In his activities as dramaturg, the interventionist helps them not only to achieve this perspective, but also to rewrite their parts, rarely if ever taking the central creative activity himself, since he is well aware that in the final analysis it is the social actor who must perform the part and do it with a considerable degree of attachment if it is to be sustained.

The Difficulties of Bringing About Change

As has been indicated in Chapter 6 it is not easy to bring about second-order change. Actors may prefer the known to the unknown and may be manipulative in their attempts to block change. By far the greatest difficulty, however, is encountered when the social actors are completely unable to see the implications of their behaviour. A major difficulty for any interventionist can arise when the actors are so deeply attached to the scripts that they are quite unable to step outside their parts and consider events metatheatrically. Such attachment is not as unusual as it may appear upon first consideration. It commonly occurs that social actors play out the 'expert script', for example, whereby it is deeply held within the organization that experts can be hired to solve problems. Thus for interpersonal problems an organization development expert is located and brought in to resolve the issues; whatever his protestations to the contrary he will be considered the expert and will be expected to make recommendations from a position of authority. Thus we have a dilemma: the interventionist as critic sees the tendency to play out the expert script as an issue in the organization but in making this point is himself cast into a similar part. The social actors engage him as they engage each other, and it may be extremely difficult for him to arrive at a position whereby the actors can become aware of this altercasting. If he struggles not to play the expert, they may consider him useless or irrelevant; if he succumbs he is part of their situational script. I am not suggesting that this is the strategy adopted by the cast of the situational script; they do not usually set out to take over the interventionist. It is simply because they are unable to conceive of any other script, it is a consequence of their deep attachment to their parts, that they cannot understand the attempts the interventionist makes to have them behave differently. His attempts to avoid the expert stance, so much a part of their interpretation, may be mistaken for weakness and incompetence and his ideas may then fail to have any impact.

For the interventionist faced with such a strong attachment to roles and to situational scripts, falling into line and playing his part as cast by them may not be the optimum course to pursue. The practice of *disengagement*, though more difficult and certainly a riskier course to pursue, may be more successful in bringing about the conditions for second-order change. Disengagement is the process whereby Alter refuses to go along with Ego's presentation of self in such a way that the act of refusal causes Ego to focus upon his own behaviour. It differs from feedback in that it doesn't provide Ego with awareness so that *he* may decide whether or not to revise his part and his scripts. Disengagement, since it does not provide Ego with the expected complementarity, pulls him up sharply.

The practice is delineated neatly by Beier (1966) and takes a number of forms. For example, after a considerable build-up of tension this interaction occurred in a T-group (all quotes from Mangham, 1977, unless otherwise indicated)

'Ego: This is just another example of your policy of divide and rule! (Very angry. Casts
        Alter into the role of one who must fight or withdraw)

Alter: Oh is it? Perhaps you would like to say more?
        (expressed in an encouraging,
        non-hostile, non-withdrawing manner)'

   In this case, Ego does not succeed in casting Alter into the situational 'fight/flight' script Ego's behaviour so often elicits. It could be that eliciting anger and rejection from others is a way of maintaining adjustment to his self-conception as a 'rejected' person. It may be important for him to push people away and to act in a hostile or aggressive manner. Alter does not fall into the part cast for him; repeated refusal to be cast into such a part by Alter *may* cause Ego to consider his own behaviour and why it is he is not achieving his ends. Through an analysis of the communication process, initiated by himself as a consequence of Alter's actions, Ego may experience how he, himself, creates and plays out particular scripts. Thus repeated refusal on the part of the interventionist to play the part of the 'expert' may lead the social actor who creates the expectation to look at his own behaviour more critically: 'Why will this chap not do what I want of him . . . perhaps it's not appropriate to expect it of him.'
   As Beier (1966) notes, there are several categories of response which may serve Alter in disengaging from Ego's expectations. The 'Hm, hm', 'Go on', 'Say more' type of response occurs in the absence of more specific forms of disengagement and provides Ego with the information that Alter is listening but that the relationship is one in which Alter is not going to give the expected responses.
   Reflecting feelings and issues back to Ego is a more specific form of disengagement and one frequently observed in interventionists:

'Ego: Much more of these pointless ramblings about relationships and values from you
        and I'm going back to work.
Alter: You feel pretty angry right now?'

   This type of reflection is disengaging since it pushes the focus back to Ego. Though not necessarily successful (it can and does sometimes generate even more anger), if persisted with it may cause Ego to look at his own anger and the causes of it.
   Probing also tends to be disengaging since questions interrupt the process of altercasting:

'Ego: I must say the argument made me feel pretty pissed off.
Alter: What do you think it did to David?'

In some sense this could better be termed *deflecting*, since it encourages Ego to eschew sympathy seeking and consider the consequence of his actions to others.

Then, in this non-exhaustive list, there is the type of response which almost parodies the role Ego is professing:

'Ego: You fellows must be in the game for the kicks you get out of it. Watching others squirm.

(said with considerable hostility)

Alter: Why else would we spend time with a chap like you?'

Technically termed the 'paradigmatic response' it consists in exaggerating Ego's way of behaving and thereby attempting to 'take the wind out of his sails' (Beier, 1966):

'Ego: What I want from you is a report which lays it out as it is, what's wrong with us and what we need to do to get it sorted out. No flambuoyant social science stuff, just the facts and the recommendations and I want it done to a tight time schedule.

Alter: Certainly. Would you like it gift wrapped or will you take it in plain covers?'

In effect, disengagement, as the word implies, breaks the usual flow of the situational script to cause Ego to examine his own behaviour. In the example above, it would be difficult for Ego to continue to cast Alter into a subservient role given the response by Alter. The disengaging response shatters the natural, taken-for-granted script so often invoked by Ego and may cause him to reflect upon it or to explore it with the interventionist in a way which feedback (a more distant, less evaluative and more 'civilized' form of disengagement) may not have brought about.

That the technique works and results in a change of behaviour (even when not mediated by awareness or reflection) is attested by Melly (1965) in his autobiography *Owning Up*:

'After the session, having no instrument to pack up, I wandered out on the steps to breathe a little air under the Mancunian stars. A young thug and his mate surrounded me and jostled me into a dark corner. One of them had a bottle, as yet unbroken, but he had begun to tap it against the wall, gradually increasing the strength of the blows. When that breaks, I thought, he's going to push it in my face. They were swerving and lunging around me to work themselves up to what they meant to do. One of them grabbed me by the lapels and gave me the head, that is butted me with his forehead. My nose started to bleed.

I was anaesthetized by fear. I subconsciously did the only thing that might work and it did. I took out of my pocket a small book of the sound poems of the dadaist Kurt Schwitters, explained what they were, and began to read. The book was knocked out of my hand but I bent and picked it up again, and read on:

Iangesturgle pi pi pi pi pi
Iangesturgle pi pi pi pi pi
Ookar
Iangesturgle pi pi pi pi pi
Ookar
Rackerterpaybee

Rackerterpaybay
Ookar
Iangesturgle pi pi pi pi pi
etc.

Slowly, muttering threats, they moved off. I can't explain why it worked, but I suspect it was because they needed a conventional response in order to give me a going over. If I'd pleaded or attempted to defend myself, or backed against the wall with my arm over my face, I think I'd have had it.' (Reproduced by permission of George Weidenfeld & Nicolson Ltd.)

That, Mr Melly, was an example of disengagement and its power in radically redefining situational scripts.

Summary

I have proposed, in these last few pages, that there are two orders of change (creatively labelled 'first' and 'second' order) and that the dramaturgical model can be useful in explaining the processes involved in each. In first-order change, the interventionist as dramaturg coaches and counsels particular actors in the situational script. Second-order change involves actors in becoming aware of the script and in rewriting it; in this case the role of the interventionist is to provide feedback or information, encourage the actors to disengage from the parts they perform and achieve a metatheatrical perspective, and assist them in rewriting their scripts and performing the new or revised parts. Much of the accepted language of organization development is not related to the dramaturgical perspective, but as I have sought to demonstrate much of the practice is explicable within it.

Chapter **9**

The Pygmalion Effect

In this part of the book I wish to present two cases of attempted change in relationships within organizations which involved me directly. The first is concerned with the activities of the senior group of managers who were introduced in an earlier chapter as they deliberated over advertising budgets. The second, an even more ambitious attempt to change a whole set of scripts within an organization, will be presented in the next chapter.

It will be recalled by those of you who have not skimped their way through this book that my friends in the mythical drug company provided the material for the illustration of situational, personal, and strategic scripts. To enable the reader to renew his or her superficial acquaintance with the social actors who will be the focus of much of the discussion in this chapter, I have reproduced below a further extract from their deliberations.

As we join them they are discussing industrial relations, which has been strategically introduced by the Industrial Relations Director under the agenda item 'Any Other Business':

HARRY: (Industrial Relations Officer) *Oh I've got, yes, I've got one thing . . . does anyone have any different views on the closed shop. The union, the Engineering Union and the Electrical Union are again approaching us on things like contracts and different things . . . that's all done, they have come again to talk about money and clothes and overalls and the closed shop, to them, you know, that's a very important thing . . . our intention is to say 'No' which is what we've said before which I'm sure has your blessing. . . .* (said in an information-passing rather than an opinion-seeking manner)

FRANK: (Head of Vioticin) *Is that 'No' that it should be no different from the USDAW agreement?*

JOHN: (Head of Tricyclin) *That's nationally negotiated.*

HARRY: *Sorry, that's nationally negotiated.*

JOHN: *I think you go on saying 'No' until the point when you can't go on saying 'No' any longer.*

ANTHONY: (Market Research Manager) *When is that? When they start working to rule . . . I mean you'll get it weekends, I mean they all want Saturdays and Sundays.*

JOHN: *Test them, test them to that point! Once you're threatened with industrial action, I mean you've got to judge it, then give way before it happens.*

ERIC: (Head of Diodin) *Well, as I see it, its a question of whether we are going to behave sensibly or not . . .* (laughs) *. . . Whether we are going to take the initiative rather than waiting for somebody to kick us and then saying 'OK. We give in'. . . . Thus merely demonstrating once again that kicking is the only way of getting somewhere. . . .* (laughs)

JOHN: (coldly) *I'm not suggesting that.*

ERIC: (backing off) *No, I know you're not, John, but that's what we are saying isn't it? I mean I really cannot see why we cannot in the name of common sense offer something to them that we've already given to USDAW. . . .*

JOHN: *Because we got something back from them. . . . I would want to know what we'd get back from them in return if we gave them this. . . .*

ANTHONY: *I'm not sure that carries much weight. I mean you can't say to them 'Well we will give you that because it was negotiated nationally'. I mean people don't think that way.*

JOHN: *Which people are we talking about. You can't talk in abstracts. The man who is doing the negotiating has got to be able to judge . . . When he's getting his head near the brick wall, when he's near the wall, when he gets the smell of the brick wall he's got to be able to judge, he's got to be able to change the whole thing so that he is seen to give rather than seen to be forced to concede.*

HARRY: *So in the end we are prepared to give in?*
(Noises of general support.)

FRANK: *And ASTMS?* (a white-collar union busily recruiting in the industry)

HARRY: *What's the point of going on hours and hours of negotiating and ending up with a fight?*

ANTHONY: *Exactly.*

FRANK: *ASTMS is the one that worries me.*

HARRY: *They haven't really mentioned it yet.*

FRANK: *But they will.*

JOHN: *They will.*

HARRY: *Our defence has been to ASTMS that this was a national negotiation, that. . . .*

CHARLES: (Managing Director) *What we must be prepared to decide then is are we prepared to risk a short work to rule . . . are we prepared to stick out and not to give in, primarily because of ASTMS rather than we are worried particularly about the craft boys.*

FRANK: *That's right . . . that would be my line. I wouldn't be too worried about the craft unions.*

ANTHONY: *There aren't many in the craft unions who don't belong.*

HARRY: *Exactly.*

ANTHONY: *A matter of about five per cent.*

CHARLES: *There might be quite a long fight.*

FRANK: *On the ASTMS one?*

CHARLES: *No, on this one because if we don't stick on this we'll get it with ASTMS. Are we prepared to have a fight?*

JOHN: *I'm not sure about a fight, but we ought to be prepared to have a tough hard negotiation. We may win, you can't start off saying we are not going to win.*

HARRY: (with force) *The trouble is there's nothing we can buy it with . . . with the pay freeze we can't put any money down to keep their minds off it . . . nothing else you can offer them . . . I mean free overalls for the closed shop it's not on.*

FRANK: *Why do they want a closed shop? . . .*

ANTHONY: *The craft union has always wanted a closed shop. It's standard procedure and they do it on the same basis that the doctors do it to protect their members in the profession. We are an exception because until now our major unions have not had a closed shop. I do not . . . I take John's point but whatever fighting talk . . . we'll give way. . . .*

HARRY: *Certainly a lot of senior people would say it's not worth the trouble, it's not worth a fight, let them have it.*

FRANK: *What, on ASTMS?*

HARRY: *Yes, a couple of your production men have talked to me.*

CHARLES: (seeking to move on) *Well, we're prepared to say that 'You'll fight as hard as you can but in the end we're prepared to give way'.*

FRANK: *Could we make sure that it is what we ought to have had with USDAW, that it is that new entrants to the company join ASTMS or whatever bit that those of our employees who are not in a union are not forced to join. I'm absolutely strong on that.*

CHARLES: *I agree with that.* (seeks to move on)

HARRY: *And then they will say, 'Well why don't you get that agreement with USDAW?'*

FRANK: *Because we weren't able to and that's the end of that . . . it really must be a sticking point.*

HARRY: (doubtfully) *well we can try and get that.*

JOHN: *It's not a case of trying, it's a sticking point.*

CHARLES: (to Harry) *You're clear you fight and in the end you give in.*

FRANK: *With this proviso, yes. . . .*

ANTHONY: *We ought to take into account that the craft unions already have a closed shop in factories just down the road.*

JOHN: *I think we've got to take into account that if there had been cases of trouble over the closed shop . . . I'm sure that USDAW would have been sympathetic . . . but in the case of. . . .*

HARRY: *There have been some . . . one coming up and they are far from being sympathetic.*

JOHN: *Now, wait a minute . . . ASTMS will not be sympathetic, and some of*

my people would rather go to the gallows than join.
FRANK: That's right.
(Silence.)
CHARLES: Any other business?

In my role as critic I spent nearly six months with this group of senior managers, talking to them individually about what they saw themselves as doing and observing them collectively as they went about running their business. In total I observed and recorded well over a hundred hours of their meetings. The extracts presented in this book, both in the earlier chapter and here, are fairly representative of the scripts they created and responded to. It will be recalled that in the advertising budgets script Eric manifested a nervousness and diffidence which, although difficult to capture on paper (the tone of voice is a crucial feature of such diffidence), is present in this extract also, particularly in his relationship to the 'angry young man', John:

JOHN: (coldly) *I'm not suggesting that*
ERIC: (backing off) *No, I know you're not, John. . . .*

Although he continues to talk he is soon effectively shut out by John and makes no further contribution. Discussion with Eric confirmed that such conflict avoidance was a personal script and one of which he had partial awareness:

ERIC: *Look, frankly, I don't think there is any point in sailing directly into
           each other. When I see someone heading across my bows, sure I'll try
           to signal to him, let him know we are on a collision course, but in the
           final analysis if he chooses to crowd on more sail and come straight at
           me I'll veer off. There's no point in barging into people just for the sake
           of it.*
SELF: *Does that mean he gets his own way?*
ERIC: *No, no. There are more ways to skin a cat. . . . Look, frankly, I think
           public squabbles get people nowhere. I'd talk about it probably with
           him—out of the meeting and we'd come to some sort of agreement.*
SELF: *Always.*
ERIC: *Frankly, Iain, in this business it can be dog eat dog and if he didn't want
           to go along with what I was suggesting I'd try to get it through round
           the back way. . . .*
SELF: *I'm not sure I. . . .*
ERIC: *I'd put it to Charles! I'd sort it out with him!*
SELF: *You'd go round the chap to the Managing Director?*
ERIC: *Yes. Look, life's too short to be involved in interminable hassles with
           one's colleagues. If it can't be sorted out without emotional blow-ups,
           yes I'd go round and straight to Charles.*

Frank, the person whose behaviour I have depicted as being controlled and strategic, was also aware of his own performance. I asked him after the meeting about his introduction of the ASTMS into the conversation. It will be recalled that immediately prior to his intervention the following exchange had occurred:

HARRY: *So in the end we are prepared to give in?*
              (Noises of general support.)
FRANK: *And ASTMS?*

He appears to be a master of the apparently innocent question, a technique we have seen him use effectively in the exchange around the advertising budgets. At first he responded with a denial of anything other than a search for information:

FRANK: *The question was nothing more or less than a request to know what we are to do if a similar request is raised by ASTMS.*
SELF: *It sounded a bit more loaded than that to me.*
FRANK: *Ah yes, but then you spend your life reading things into questions and comments.* (laughs) *OK. Yes. If we are to get anywhere I've got to be reasonably open with you haven't I? I don't think we've thought our ideas through on any union issue and I certainly don't think we've done a good job in thinking about the ASTMS. . . .*
SELF: *So.*
FRANK: *So I asked about it. I drew attention to the fact that there we were all saying 'yes', yes' to the engineers and the craft unions and none of us was thinking about the implications of that for relations with ASTMS.*
SELF: *You were not seeking to confuse the issue?*
FRANK: (spreading his hands laughs) *Me? Me? Now whatever gave you that idea? You have got a nasty suspicious mind! No, look I think we need to be clear, we need to have some sort of policy. You know we never really discuss things like this properly. Yes, I suppose, I was at some level trying to block a decision. . . . I want us to think about it. . . .*

Both Anthony, the Market Research Manager, and John the aggressive Head of Trycyclin were, to differing degrees, aware of their personal scripts as well as of the scripts of others:

JOHN: *Frank knows what he is doing. If you watch him you realize that every so often he drops something in—just to muddy the water as it were. . . .*

He was equally articulate about his own script:

JOHN: *I'm a noisy, aggressive sod. It's the only way to get something done around here. To be honest with you it's not just here—my brother keeps telling me I'd be better off and live longer if I just stopped shouting, showed a bit more patience and tolerance. Trouble is I cannot suffer fools gladly. . . . Actually I can't suffer fools at all!*

Anthony, much more long-winded and more cerebral, considered himself to be 'somewhat difficult to understand':

ANTHONY: *I find it difficult to get my points across. They don't seem to have any impact on some or even most of my colleagues. Harry sometimes goes along with me, but most often I'm alone, crying in the wilderness.* (laughs) *A prophet without honour you know. . . . I don't know what to do about it, I don't know how I can get them to listen.*

And so on. I talked with each manager about his personal script, the scripts he saw others following, and the situational script of what became known as the Friday meeting. There was very little attachment to this particular meeting:
  'Just a talking shop, really. We never really decide anything.'
  'It ought to be about policy. It ought to be about long-term thinking. Instead it degenerates into wrangles about operations.'
  'Bloody waste of time, most weeks.'
  'We don't really thrash anything out. We often leave not knowing what it is we've agreed.'
  'Well, we do pass some information around but we do very little else.'

Having completed my observations I convened an off-site meeting of the group. I introduced the idea of personal and situational scripts to them and said that for the purposes of this particular session I would be feeding back my views of the Friday meeting and inviting them to comment upon them. I stated that unless they expressed a wish to the contrary I would restrict my comments on personal scripts to the minimum necessary to illustrate basic points. I invited them to place themselves in the role of critic at a first night and to distance themselves from the material they were about to hear. I made some introductory comments about the way the data had been collected and analysed stressing the essentially subjective nature of my review, and then began the feedback by presenting a *pot-pourri* of their views on the Friday meeting much as they are presented above—raw quotes with no identification.

The impact was considerable. Amazingly, few if any of them had ever revealed their views on the meeting to each other. Initially there was a considerable amount of laughter and some half-hearted attempts to identify the particular quotes. Subsequently there was a lively discussion of the shortcomings of the meeting with many assertions of how it ought to be conducted and for what ends. These views and ideas were recorded in newsprint to be used later 'to rewrite the script'.

I focused their attention on some of the specific features of their present situational scripts by playing to them extracts from the tape similar to that presented above and those presented in the earlier chapter. Again these were received with a degree of incredulity the first time they were played:

  'Did I actually say that?'

'We don't appear to listen to each other do we?'
'God, I waffle on don't I?'

We played the extracts several times and in true democratic fashion I sought to involve them in the analysis. They had difficulty in recognizing what it was I was after, tending to look rather at the personalities involved in particular discussions rather than at the patterns of interaction the extracts revealed. After prompting, however, they became sufficiently detached to be able to discern conflict-avoidance scripts, leader-deferral scripts, and the like. In short, they were able to adopt the metatheatrical perspective and review critically their own interactions.

By the second day we moved on to the rewrite stage. We had agreed that the present scripts were less than optimum either for personal satisfaction or organizational effectiveness and we had agreed that most of us had had a hand in maintaining the situation in its current, less than satisfactory, state. Utilizing ideas deriving from Benne and Sheats' (1948) list of role functions in a group, we focused on the parts that needed to be played in order to make the group more effective and considered the implications of these in terms of the future conduct of the Friday meetings. The role of the chairman of the meeting had been subjected to some scrutiny and it had been concluded that his current performance based upon *laissez-faire* ideas was not to everyone's liking. It was suggested to him that, while they did not want him to assume total responsibility for the conduct of the meetings, they did look to him to exercise more control than heretofore. Charles explained that his performance to date had been influenced by his desires to give everyone a chance to speak; he was, he said, fearful that his position and his authority might stifle the expression of opinion. He was told that, on the contrary, his failure to pass an opinion or to provide a sense of direction only led to speculation about what he might be thinking or wanting. Most thought they would prefer a situation in which he participated more fully.

The meeting concluded, as most such meetings conclude in my experience, with loud protestations to do better and to work more effectively together in the brave new world which now confronted them. And there it might have ended had I not been committed to a dramaturgical perspective on the changing of relationships.

In effect, at that stage, we had little more than a desire to perform differently. Certainly the social actors had more awareness of what they had been doing to each other and the insight so achieved had led to a desire to change. We were like a company of actors, however, with nothing more than dissatisfaction with their present scripts and a sketchy outline of a revised script. In the absence of anything else the actors, in my opinion, would have been more than likely to revert to their old parts.

I took it upon myself to work intensely with the individual actors, have them look at their personal scripts as well as the parts they played out in the Friday meeting situational scripts. I reviewed with them each individually the discussions we had had together and drew to their attention the specific patterns they contributed to and to which they responded within the meetings. For example, I meet with Charles before each of the Friday meetings and went through the agenda with him urging him to consider what he wanted out of the meeting. Was it a discussion? A decision? Or advice so that he could make the decision? I coached him carefully and extensively in the skills of drawing people into the discussion, clarifying issues, summarizing, and putting issues to a test for consensus. After each meeting we reviewed what we had done and how. Often as a consequence of his actions patterns of behaviour had been different. Both before and after the meetings we literally improvised and rehearsed the kinds of words and phrases which Charles would or could have used and, between us, we acted out the consequences of particular scripts.

I worked in a similar fashion with Eric, discussing with him his personal script, particularly his tendency to create and then rapidly retreat from conflict. Before each meeting I urged him to consider his own interests and to articulate as clearly as possible the outcome he could personally find satisfying. Together we tried to forecast the potential areas of conflict and together we simulated or rehearsed the form the interaction may take. Eric both in his out-of-town trial runs, as it were, and to a great extent in his actual performances within the group meetings reduced his displays of nervousness and diffidence. He could still be blown off course by a particularly sharp report from John but, by and large, his performance was seen by him and, somewhat ruefully, by others to have become more congruent. When he made a point he did not immediately withdraw it by laughing or by conveying non-verbally that he would be content to have it ignored.

John was a much more difficult person to work with. His attitude was brusque and dismissive. 'Look, Iain, it's a tough world and those who can't take it should get out.' In general he felt that aggression and competitive behaviour were 'in most cases appropriate; it's dog eat dog here'. Although very aware of his impact on others he considered that it was up to them to change and learn to fight him more effectively; the notion of him helping them he found 'odd'. His stance towards me throughout our initial discussions had the same challenging, argumentative tone that he adopted towards his colleagues, and it was only when I began to gently chide him and to refer to him as the Mussolini of the management team that we began to have different conversations:

JOHN: *Mussolini? Why Mussolini?*
SELF: *You remember him don't you, or was he before your time? Short fat chap with a bald head, Italian dictator, always huffing and puffing . . . .*
JOHN: *All wind and piss.*
SELF: *You said it, not me.*
JOHN: *That's what you are getting at aren't you? You reckon I'm full of wind don't you?*
SELF: *Not full but pretty well inflated at times. . . .*
JOHN: *OK. OK. So I make a lot of noise over very little sometimes but it's the only way . . . .You've got to be heard in this place.*

SELF: *It might help to hear as well, occasionally . . . .*

It would be nice to report that John did moderate his tone of voice, did add other skills to his repertoire such as listening and helping others to make their points. It would be nice but, unfortunately, untrue. Although we discussed a new personal script and to a limited extent developed one between ourselves it was never performed on the stage of the Friday meeting. John did, however, cease to dominate the proceedings. In effect by remaining silent for longer periods than he had been accustomed to he gave people such as Anthony and Eric more opportunity to air their ideas.

Anthony, too, was a focus of coaching. He rapidly recognized and openly acknowledged his lack of impact; he had even raised it at the off-site meeting only to have it powerfully confirmed since no one else considered it worth discussing! I worked with him over a period of some three months, helping him to clarify the patterns of behaviour he both created and responded to and helping him to develop new scripts. Since much of his impact upon the group was related to the written briefs he prepared for them, we worked together on writing some which put his ideas across cogently and without excessive qualification, since we recognized the force of comments elicited from other members that 'he is long-winded and overintellectualizes'. Anthony worked hard at presenting himself in a more concise and assertive fashion and found that as the weeks went by he was being paid more and more attention.

Thus with a number of the actors I consciously and deliberately sought to encourage them to take a strategic perspective on the Friday meeting. I urged them to consider what purposes and intentions they had and I coached them in performing well the parts they identified they wanted to play. Clearly the parts they undertook were the product of discussion and were informed by my views on what I saw to be more effective performances both for the individual actors and for the group as a whole. As dramaturg I had the entire play in mind and my separate rehearsals were geared to a final ensemble performance every Friday afternoon. During the week I was a very central figure; on Friday I watched and waited in the wings as the cast realized their scripts.

In the short run there can be no doubt that the effort was worth while. A number of the actors began to see the meetings as much more productive and to see the performances of themselves and their colleagues as contributing to this improvement.

I say in the short run because a number of factors conspired to bring about the demise of the activity. First, and perhaps most significantly, pressure to extend the work in the company meant that the amount of time I had for coaching and discussion was limited. Second, the demands on the time of the social actors made it difficult for them to rehearse for the Friday meeting and, third, there were changes in the personalities involved, both Eric and John being promoted elsewhere in the group.

I attended the meetings occasionally in this later period and very occasionally had a pre or post session with Charles, the Managing Director. Even without the constant attention there still remained some of the features we had so earnestly agreed as being desirable at our feedback session. There was, however, a falling-away, a tendency to slide back into confusion and disarray which was disappointing. The play, it seems, if it is to have a long run needs periodic reexamination to reinvigorate it.

Chapter 10

Eating Your Elephant a Spoonful at a Time

As French and Bell (1973) note, team-building activities are probably the most important single group of interventions undertaken by organizational development practitioners. Sooner or later, however, many of us aspire to move beyond the one-act play to tackle the epic drama, the total organization intervention. Given the present state of our understanding and our current technology, such aspirations may be dangerous—a case of 'vaulting ambition which o'er leaps itself'.

Nonetheless, there are a number of examples of organization-wide interventions in the literature (Beckhard, 1969; Blake and Mouton, 1969; Marrow, Bowers, and Seashore, 1967), not all of which may be deemed overambitious. Apart from the scale of the operation, organization-wide intervention differs from team building (which may, of course, be subsumed in the former) in the length of time that it takes to bring about change. For the interventionist D'Aprix's (1972) caution needs to be taken to heart; he argues that such a person must be prepared to work beyond the failures of today to the probable successes of tomorrow. 'Fortitude,' he writes, 'is not much in fashion any more, but unless you can eat your elephant a spoonful at a time, life in the organization can become very depressing.'

What follows is a brief account of 'elephant eating' which took place over three years and which had its share of failures and successes, frustration and fortitude.

Twilight Electronics Ltd

Twilight Electronics is part of a large group of British companies operating in the provision of electronic components for calculators, television sets, microwave ovens, and other pieces of relatively sophisticated equipment. At the time it employed around six hundred people, many of whom were graduate development engineers engaged in work for the particular factory involved in the change project and in work for other factories belonging to the group. The factory was relatively new to the group, having been acquired in a recent takeover, and many of the employees appeared to prefer their previous identity to the new one arising from the merger, though, at the beginning of the intervention, there had been few changes in direction or management style.

The decision to conduct an organization-wide change programme arose out of the rejection of a small-scale study by the present author. At the invitation of the Factory Manager I had conducted a number of interviews with several of the key actors in the organization and had identified a number of problems mostly of an interpersonal and intergroup nature. My critical review of the organizational scripts sustained by these individuals and their groups was not well received by any of the parties concerned. In the feeding back of the results of my interviews and observations I was unable to promote the necessary metatheatrical perspective; nor was I able to disengage from the patterns of behaviour so typical of the organization as I had at that time seen it. A number of my comments had to do with the hostility which informed the relation of the Production Manager and the Research and Development Director and the tension which existed between their departments; both denied the hostility and, in effect, joined forces in seeking to expel me and deny the basis of my critical review. The Factory Manager, an equally aggressive character if not such a hostile one, acknowledge that there 'may be' something in what I was saying, but was strongly critical of the way the material had been collected and presented. The essence of his criticism was that my approach was 'subjective', 'impressionistic', and 'unsystematic'. What he and his colleagues wanted, albeit with less enthusiasm, was a more 'objective, quantified approach'. For an aspiring dramaturg such words sound a frightful note; it's somewhat like asking a playwright to spend his time providing grocery lists. Nonetheless, since we needed the work I and two colleagues accepted the brief 'to investigate the organizational structure and process (at that time we preserved the distinction) of Twilight Electronics and, after consideration of certain unavoidable constraints imposed by membership of a group of companies, to assist in the generation, initiation and implementation of improvements in the structure and process'.

We decided that an appropriate methodology meeting the criteria of relative objectivity, quantitative measures, and systematic data collection, and yet still relating to the basic dramaturgical framework, could be derived from role theory, notably the work of Gross, Mason, and McEachern (1958) and Kahn *et al.* (1964) From this perspective organizational life can be seen to consist of roles and role-related behaviour. If any particular role is taken as focal, other roles which relate to it can be identified and measures of ambiguity, tension, conflict, pressure to change behaviour, and so on, can be constructed—all very quantitative and superficially objective.

To manage the programme a steering group was formed consisting of people operating the most powerful groups in the organization. In effect, this was the management team since the plant was non-unionized. This group was to meet once a month under the chairmanship of the Factory Manager and with the attendance of all three of the interventionists.

The steering group was to be regarded not as an optional extra but as an integral part of the model of change. It was not just that sanction was required from the highest levels of management, the kind of benevolent apathy expected of them by many change programmes, but that their actual participation was needed in the process.

Within the plant and including members of the Steering Group ninety-one people were chosen and treated as occupying focal positions. These people were given a face-to-face interview. The interview consisted of formulating a list of activities comprising the job of the focal role and also enumerating a role set and choosing some ten members of this role set to represent the complete set. The person being interviewed was asked to answer questions concerning each of the ten or so members of the role set. These questions concerned both the quality of the interpersonal relationship and the work-related aspects of the relationship. In effect we were seeking to tap both personal and situational scripts. The interview also included questions concerning the ambiguity and tension experienced by the person occupying the focal role.

The ten or so people mentioned by the person occupying the focal role were then given a questionnaire. The so-called 'role sender questionnaire' was oriented towards finding the pressures for change concerning the focal role. This questionnaire had two aspects, as did the focal interview, that is to say, an interpersonal component and a work-related component.

Because of research demands a uniform coverage to all the organization was given. That is to say, more information was not collected where there appeared to be problems and less information where the opposite applied. This meant that a great deal of information was never used. On the other hand it had the advantage of making the investigation more exhaustive and internally comparative. Some questions had relevance only for research purposes, but most, if not directly associated with one of the behavioural measures mentioned later, were useful in building up cases prior to the problem-recognition stage (see Figure 3). Most of the behavioural measures used were symptom descriptive rather than problem descriptive, and hence the explorative problem-recognition stage was a necessary part of the process.

The measures used in the interview and questionnaire material were derived from role theory (Kahn *et al.*, 1964), but were used to try to gain understanding of how individual actors as focal office holders defined their situations and how related actors sought to influence the behaviour of the office holder. Role-analysis methodology was adopted since it had some respectability in terms of validity and reliability, but throughout the investigation emphasis was upon seeking to understand the dynamics of interaction within the organization rather than simply forcing answers into a systematic predetermined research framework.

The more formal measures adopted were:

(1) *Tension* This measure attempted to indicate the anxiety and some of the stress experienced by the individual concerned. Both people occupying focal positions and role senders completed the questions which were used to compute this index; thus departmental and individual measures could be taken for the tension index.

(2) *Ambiguity* This index had two components: first, a role-related component which dealt with the certainty of the individual, the expectations of those

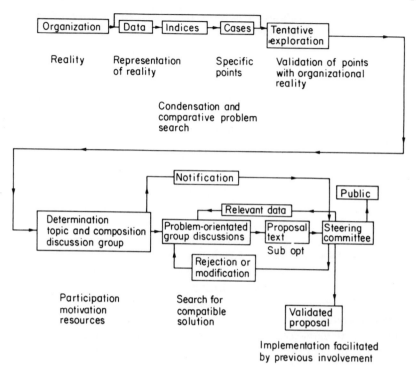

Figure 3

people comprising his role set; second, an introspective component signifying the uncertainty the individual felt about his own role.

(3) *Affective bonds index* This dealt with the aspects of liking, trust, and respect which the focal expressed for his role set.

(4) *Ideational conflict* This dealt with the pressure on the focal role by the role set change in his activities.

(5) *Temporal activity conflict* This dealt with the pressures for greater or lesser amounts of time to be spent on the various activities comprising the job of the focal role.

(6) *Interpersonal change pressure* This dealt with the changes of interpersonal style that the role set wished to see in the person occupying the focal role.

(7) *Interpersonal ideal conflict* This was obtained by the discrepancy between the description of the ideal person and the actual person occupying the focal role as perceived by the role set.

At a less formal level:

Job satisfaction This measure attempted to find the satisfaction obtained by the individual in his job. Along with the questionnaire which purported to measure job satisfaction, another questionnaire concerning job reorganization was given out to individuals. This proved to be a rich source of ideas and dissatisfaction with the present system.

The Action Stage of the Exercise

The action stage of the exercise is represented in diagrammatic form in Figure 3. This indicates how the data were processed and utilized. Working from left to right across the diagram, the organization is represented by the role-theoretical data. These data were condensed into numerical indices of the variables mentioned above. This enabled a series of individual and departmental rankings to be taken along each of the indices used. This in turn enabled case studies to be built up comprising aspects from all the indices. The case studies were then checked against the organizational 'reality' by holding problem-recognition-and-definition meetings. In these meetings the problem was validated by the members of the organization concerned and defined in as specific a manner as possible. This problem definition was then submitted to the Steering Committee. Discussion groups were then held which had a problem-solving orientation. The objective of these groups was to forward a proposal which was designed to tackle the problem as previously defined. These proposals were submitted to the Steering Committee for validation and subsequent implementation.

In this way we had access to and caused the members of the organization to focus upon a number of situational scripts and a few key performances. Over the three years we discussed and sought to modify in association with the social actors' scripts concerned with:

(1) The transition of devices between the development and production functions
(2) The operation of the mechanical engineering department
(3) Advanced planning
(4) The circulation of targets
(5) Production information
(6) Communication of performance results
(7) Responsibility for advanced devices
(8) Appraisal systems
(9) Grading and salary awards

An example of the kind of work we were involved in may be derived from the first of the items listed above: the transition of devices from development to production.

The earlier survey had indicated strong interpersonal conflict between the Development Manager and the Production Manager which derived not only from interface problems of their areas of responsibility but also from ambition. Both were seen to be in line for the Factory Manager's job should he move on. There was little that could be done about this aspect of the situation other than to indulge in a degree of counselling and process consultation with the two of them.

The approach to the interdepartmental conflict was less interpersonal, more task oriented, and, in the end, rather more structural.

The role-related indices confirmed a high degree of tension, conflict, and ambiguity around the transition interface between development and production. Discussions further confirmed the symptoms of the problem and a project group was set up to further define it and to develop and implement some solutions. This project team, like all the others consisted of representatives of those internally involved in the problem plus one of the interventionists.

The historical organizational situation had been that development transferred devices to production on an appointed day or at a predetermined point when sufficient numbers had been manufactured under development auspices to required quality standards. This direct development-to-production transition was found to be suited to the new device types where the device was relatively 'simple' in concept and where the device technology was already well established within the production department. Where the device itself was more complex and, more importantly, where new technologies were being introduced into production for the first time, a great deal of conflict and ambiguity about responsibility was engendered. Production men in many cases recognized that they did not have the technical ability to solve the problems with the devices and called upon development engineers who sometimes responded by pointing out it was no longer their concern. Other production men took it upon themselves to solve the technical problems and, according to the development men, merely compounded them.

Thus each party to the problem variously defined the situation as one which did not include the others, some production men presented themselves as competent, others as less so, and, in so doing, each cast the development engineer in a role appropriate to their own idiosyncratic definition and acted accordingly.

The amount of ambiguity, tension, and conflict surrounding this particular interface was evidence of the fragility and instability of the negotiated order. No one from device to device was quite sure who should be doing what, when, and with whom. Initial discussions were heated and characterized by attempts to assign blame to one party or the other. One meeting broke up in disarray after a development engineer accused his production counterpart of 'incompetence' and 'sheer bloody ignorance'. The interventionist eventually persuaded the two groups—development and production men—separately to consider the problems in role terms: leaving aside for the moment who should do it, what needs to be done to make the transition more effective? What pattern of activities and what order of events are necessary? The definitions arrived at by the two groups were similar enough for a joint meeting to be convened which produced an agreed pattern of activities, a revised script, and an agreed assignment of parts.

In the process of discussion it was recognized that there could be no one best way to handle the transition period of devices since the definitions, needs, self-images, and aspirations of members of the two groups differed. What the joint meeting eventually produced was a framework for the negotiation of order with respect to device transfer, a set of ground rules, or considerations which were to be taken into account in coming to an arrangement about responsibility and involvement in the varying phases of device development and production. What follows is an extract from the joint proposal to the Steering Committee:

'1. In an ideal situation, when a perfect development exercise has been carried out, it should only be necessary to transfer a set of process instructions, drawings and inspection instructions across to production to enable them to manufacture the device. This idealised situation is never achieved in practice. Problems arise in production or pre-production which were not foreseen in the development phase, and in many cases can only be solved by the engineer responsible for the development. Thus in any transfer situation as well as the transfer of documentary information, the development engineer concerned must be available for problem solving during the initial production phase. Accepting this fact, it is the various modes of employment of this engineer that has been under general discussion in past months.

1.1. In discussions on how to optimise the transfer of information and engineering know-how from Development to Production several factors must be taken into consideration.

1.1i. Is it optimum for the factory as a whole?

1.1ii. Is it optimum for the Development and Production departments?

1.1iii. Is it optimum for the device?

1.1iv. Is it acceptable by the engineer?

1.2. Taking 1.1iii *in isolation* it may well be that the simplest and most effective method of transferring technical know-how is to transfer the development engineer with his specialised knowledge into the Production department as the line supervisor. Taking the other factors into consideration, however, there can be many arguments against this being the accepted and only possible method. It is, however, possible that when all the conditions mentioned in 1.1i–1.1iv are acceptable then this method of transfer of technical know-how could be adopted.

2. *Existing and Proposed Transfer Schemes* can be summarised below:

2.1. *Direct Development to Production*

2.1i. *Existing*

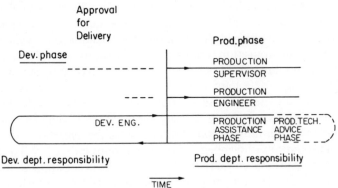

2.1ii. *Proposed additional to above in agreed cases*

(see 1.1i. to 1.1iv)

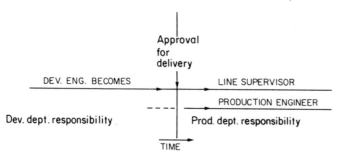

2.2. *Development—Pre-production—Production*
  2.2i.

Dev. Phase	Pre-prod. Phase	Prod. Phase
	Approval for Delivery	Release for Prόduction
DEV. ENG.		
		TECH.ADVICE
	PROD. SUPERVISOR	
		PROD. ENG.
Development Dept. Responsibility		Prod. Dept. Responsibility

TIME

2.2ii.

Dev. Phase	Pre-prod. Phase	Prod. Phase
	App. for Delivery	Release for Prod.
MOMENT OF DECISION	DEV. ENG. BECOMES	LINE SUPERVISOR
	PROD. ENGINEER	
Development Dept. Responsibility		Prod. Dept. Responsibility

Figure 4

General Comments

The proposed additional schemes do not affect the basic system of transferring devices from Development to Production, but merely change the patterns of "flow" of the personnel involved. It must be emphasised that these schemes are only options open to the departments to consider and would not be operable unless all the conditions mentioned in 1.1. are favourable. The only requirement—assuming that favourable conditions exist—is to ensure that the decision to proceed with the scheme is taken in the development phase, to ensure that the Production engineer may be brought in a little earlier than normal to support the Development cum Supervisor in the pre-production phase.

General reaction from device department engineers has indicated that few might be interested in proceeding along the Development Engineer to Production Supervisor path but they all feel the scheme should exist for those who, in future, might wish to be considered.

It was also intended that the "additional" scheme might be operated in reverse, in that suitable production supervisors and/or engineers might transfer to development to follow through a development project until re-transferred with their device back to Production. Again the number of suitable candidates for the activities would not be large.'

It is clear that what was being recommended were some of the parameters and some of the elements of the script which warrant attention in deciding who is to do what. Such parameters and elements become part of the scene as defined by each individual actor, and instead of it being either my job or his, other possibilities present themselves. It is equally clear that no hard-and-fast rules were being recommended and that room for exploration and negotiation was an integral feature of the framework. Although ambiguity, tension, and conflict are potentially reduced by the adoption of the negotiating framework, they were not eliminated.

Thus this particular set of actors came together over a span of three months (1) to explicitly bring into the open the kinds of situational scripts within which they were operating, (2) to critically review these scripts and the performances arising from them, and (3) to rewrite and rehearse the elements of a different mutually more satisfying script.

The successful resolution of many of the task-related interface problems was the reward for their willingness and ability to confront openly and collaboratively the issue that has rankled between the departments for some years. The utilization of a preproduction department under development control and the increased flexibility of both production and development engineers in following through or anticipating devices had a major business impact on the organization.

A similar approach to interpreting, negotiating, and performing was used throughout the factory with varying degrees of success. Where the issues had less of an interpersonal intensity, the approach worked relatively well; where the issues covered style and interpersonal process the approach was less successful.

In making their interpretations of these scenes members of the organization tended to discount personal factors as being either irrelevant' or 'things that nothing can be done about'. In other words, going back to the initial model, their interpretations indicated to them that personal relations were irrelevant or intractable and they therefore excluded such considerations from their re-hearsals. In technical discussions participants, although frequently initially unwilling, eventually arrived at a negotiated meaning for events and situations which often subsumed differing interpretations. On interpersonal issues, how-ever, it was frequently the interventionist rather than the participants who sought to enlarge or reorient interpretations, and the strong, overriding cultural script that such factors were inappropriate or intractable proved difficult to redefine. In other words an overall factor in each individual's definition was that technical matters were negotiable and personal characteristics were not, or, more fundamentally, were not part of the reality as defined by them.

Nonetheless, the questionnaire and interviews forced people to attempt to define their own role and relationships. Aided by the structured form of interviews it is possible that many were able to express more clearly the relation between themselves and the organizational environment. People were also asked to comment critically on their role set, the people with whom they had most contacts. Again this must have clarified a whole range of evaluative feelings about others. Further, while applying such evaluation to others, it was only natural that many would have applied the critical apparatus to themselves and attempted to see themselves as others saw them. Thus it was widely accepted that people became more aware of themselves, their role and their relationships, their scripts, and a great deal of corrective activity was self-initiated.

The action stage of the exercise, involving problem identification and problem-solving groups also had a strong beneficial effect:

'People try to build real working relationships now instead of fighting.'
'The exercise has drawn people's attention to the fact that they do not work in isolation.'
'. . . People think more about problems and tend to get together more.'
'Things are much more open now—before we would just moan amongst our-selves, now we know that he (the boss) knows as well—it's cleared the air.'
'People tend to be more outspoken.'
'There is more sharing of problems.'

The group discussions apparently encouraged (1) attempts to define problems rather than just complaining, (2) a decrease in anxiety when problems are shared and brought into the open, (3) awareness of the resources available when a group as opposed to an individual attempts a solution, and (4) finally, a view that the spontaneous definition and solution of problems is not only a legitimate activity but an individual's responsibility.

As will be recalled From figure 3 and our earlier discussion the role of the organization study steering committee was vital to the whole exercise. Predictably this direct meeting was occasionally the scene of misunderstanding and strong differences of opinion. These difficulties were predictable because the exercise did literally have to be steered and directed over the course of the three years and some members did not approve of it. During this period the committee moved from suspicion of the approach to a degree of sensitive commitment. Naturally the commitment varied from member to member and, even, from meeting to meeting. The Head of Management Services remained opposed to the study throughout the period although he made few attempts to block it, whereas the Personnel Manager, while professing belief and enthusiasm for the process, made covert but concerted attempts to reduce its impact. Throughout most of the period the consultants found themselves having to defend the work in the meetings with the steering committee. It proved extremely difficult to confront these issues. Our concern for the overall impact of the work often led us not to deal with interpersonal conflicts and lack of openness in as productive or forceful a way as, in restrospect, was necessary.

Advantages of the Approach

As I have indicated, we began the project with some disdain for the systematic, quantitative approach which was urged upon us. To our surprise aspects of it proved to be advantageous. For example, by means of Figure 3 and a verbal explanation of it we were able to make a clear presentation to the members of the organization about the procedure to be followed in the programme of change. We were able to demonstrate that the model had as its implicit values a belief in the expression and sharing of problems, in participation, and in the effectiveness of group commitment and group problem solving. These value assumptions are rational and minimal. They are rational in terms of utilizing those connected with the problems in defining the problems and proposing solutions to them. They are minimal in the sense that they do not necessarily imply a wider shift towards participative management for day-to-day functioning but can be confined to exceptional problems.

Both of these views, however, were challenged. It was more 'rational' to call upon experts to solve problems in the view of some managers—notably the Head of Management Services. And some managers and staff, particularly the more junior, saw participation as a day-to-day possibility.

A further advantage of the approach was that the questionnaires and interviews based on the ideas of roles and scripts were generally seen to provide members of the organization with a vocabulary and a relatively comprehensive framework for describing their interactions. Thus an increase in self and other awareness was a general important characteristic of the change programme, which resulted primarily from a coherently related set of questions.

In transferring from a set of indices which reflect high role conflict to a problem-defining discussion it was possible to confront the person occupying the focal role with his critical role set. It was possible, that is, to present some numerical representation of the degree of dissatisfaction and lack of attachment members felt with and towards a particular situational script. Such an approach has ethical problems which had to be resolved by consent, but it does provide an efficient means of using the data.

Clearly such an approach prosecuted over three years requires considerable fortitude. As I have indicated, we had our share of little successes and large failures. Overall we did not succeed in doing more than sketch in the broad outlines of new scripts as, for example, at the production and development interface. In many areas there was strong resistance to our attempts to define, let alone seek to resolve, personal scripts insofar as these impacted upon situational scripts. In some instances, regrettably very few, we were able to help the parties to a particular script to carefully consider it and equally carefully reconstruct it. We certainly generated a great deal of data and we clearly worked through the organization systematically. It is, however, unlikely that our efforts had any lasting effects on the organization since, after three years, we had barely eaten more than half a dozen spoonfuls of our elephant.

Chapter 11

Pawns, Players, and Creative Anarchists

Throughout this book an attempt has been made to describe some of the basic elements of a framework for understanding the processes of organizational analysis and development. It is my belief that attention to microsociological concepts, notably to the processes of face-to-face interaction, is of more benefit to the would-be interventionist than is time and energy devoted to such macrosociological concepts as technology and environment.

In outline, the set of ideas I have proposed (or, rather, since few are original, I have assembled) is quite simple. Scripts provide the general pattern of parts and 'lines' within which face-to-face interaction takes place. This interstructured behaviour reduces equivocality, enables social actors to meet needs they would be unable to meet alone, and provides a degree of coordination among actors without which social life would be a teeming, buzzing confusion.

I have argued that such situational scripts arise out of circumstances where the actor's original construction of his performance becomes predictably and regularly interrelated with that of other social actors. This capacity for the construction of performance, as opposed to the unreflecting playing of parts, I have termed strategic interaction and have argued that it is an important element in the development and transformation of situational scripts. In the terms used by Watzlowick Weakland, and Fisch (1974):

'It obviously makes a difference whether we consider ourselves as pawns in a game whose rules we call reality or as players of the game who know that the rules are "real" only to the extent that we have created or accepted them, and that we can change them.'

The dramaturgical perspective thus allows for both response and initiative on the part of the social actor. As a performer within a particular situational script, the broad dimensions of his performance are outlined by custom and practice, his moves are plotted for him, and his lines marked down in the prompt book. Nonetheless there are few situational scripts which so thoroughly constrain the social actor that he is reduced to the status of a pawn. Many scripts appear to leave some opportunities for strategic interaction on the part of the participants, and a number of them leave considerable room. At the point of selection of scripts and at the point of movement from one script to another, considerable opportunities for strategic interaction appear to be open to social actors. Intervention consists of coaching the actors to play the parts better or of capitalizing upon their capacity for strategic interaction, and, by urging the actors to utilize it in achieving a metatheatrical perspective, affording them the opportunity to revise their performances, construct new parts, and whole new scripts, if desired. Thus the emphasis is upon choice.

The possibility of choice, the achievement of the metatheatrical perspective, is facilitated by the activities of the interventionist as critic. He presents his review of situational scripts and performances to the actors, comments from his own experience, and invites the actors to join in the analysis. His other activity, as dramaturg or theatrical odd-job man, is to respond to the actors' needs for revisions in the script or coaching in their parts. In carrying out this aspect of his job he contributes his own expertise but, recognizing that the performance must be an expression of the actor's self-concept if it is to be credible, he encourages the actor to find himself, as it were, and clearly to negotiate scripts which are rewarding to that self.

In sum, the ideas expressed in these pages highlight the fact that an adequate diagnosis or analysis of social relations within organizations must take into account both the situational script, the taken-for-granted social force of these relationships, and the interpretation/strategic interactions of the social actors operating within the scripts. Any social action may be seen as shaped by both of these elements.

The duality implied here is derived from and underwritten by the work of sociologists such as Goffman (1959, 1969) who has written about both 'rules' and 'strategic interaction' and by the work of anthropologists such as Geetz who has written extensively on 'not just "grammar" or "structure", but the "rhetoric" of life, not just the rules of the game but the many, often conflicting purposes people hope to realize by playing the game and the strategies and tactics (including cheating) by which they try to realize them' (Goodenough, 1974).

This duality is at the heart of the model of change proposed in these pages; man, the social actor, both competes and cooperates, is both independent and interdependent, is at once selfish and altruistic, takes a willing part in established social scripts, and is equally willing to adopt a strategic posture towards others.

Such an ambivalence is fundamental to the dramaturgical model; the actor is interested in the selection of the script in which he may shine, the cultivation of his own performance, but recognizes that he cannot devote himself exclusively to these activities since, in order to perform at all, he needs other actors. Both strategic interaction and the acceptance of situational scripts are necessary attributes of social life; without the former we would have dull, lifeless, monotonous, automatic performances and without the latter a series of tiresome monologues. On the one hand, we have the circumstance in which too ready an acceptance of the accommodation arrived at by the actors leads to stagnation and inertia; on the other, circumstances in which no accommodation leads to a breakdown of the encounter.

The Relation of the Dramaturgical Perspective to Other Models

The presentation of the duality ought, in my estimation, to be a key feature of organization development. Adaptation to change is faciliated by the encouragement of tendencies both to complete *and* to cooperate. Alternative interpretations and performances are to be welcomed, not reduced, by processes of consensus seeking at all costs. Unfortunately much of what passes for current theory and practice in organization development appears to be characterized by a desire to reduce the impact of individual performances. In Tannenbaum and Davis (1969) terms, there is a move 'away from a primary emphasis upon competition toward a much greater emphasis on collaboration'. Such a move leads to an emphasis upon the 'truth/love' model as the most appropriate method for effecting organizational change. As Winn (1971) puts it: 'Most of the organization development practitioners rely almost exclusively on . . . the "truth–love" model based on the assumption that man is reasonable and caring and that once trust is achieved, the desired social change within the organization will take place with no other source of influence required.' The model is characterized by Schmuck and Miles (1971) as a 'tender' model which 'states that shared expectations involving trust, warmth, and supportiveness are formed as the members of a working team gain confidence and skill in communicating clearly and openly. These norms and skills, in turn, support collaborative problem-solving and the rational use of information in making decisions.'

Such a model (and its associated methodology) is based upon a couple of implicit assumptions: one, that there is the possibility of a shared, unitary goal and, second, that if only open communication can be established good relationships will lead directly to the attainment of the identified unitary goal. The dramaturgical model makes no such assumption; indeed, as has been seen, it stresses that there are likely to be competing definitions of the situation, competing needs, and competing repertoires. It assumes, that is, pluralism rather than unitarism. Furthermore, it does not lead directly to an emphasis upon clear communication and authentic interpersonal relations; unlike Wesker (1960), it does not hold that words are bridges always leading to the promised land of understanding:

'Beatie:
    . . . And so sometimes when he was in a black mood he'd start on me. "What can you talk of?" he'd ask. "Go on, pick a subject. Talk. Use the language. Do you know what language is?" Well, I'd never thought before—have you?—it's automatic to you isn't it, like walking? "Well, language is words" he'd say, as though he were telling me a secret. "It's bridges so you can get from one place safely to another. And the more bridges you know about, the more places you can see!"'

The emphasis the dramaturgical perspective places upon strategic interaction indicates that the words may be used as bridges, or as weapons, or as mystifiers. Words and relationships are utilized (or, at least, are available for utilization) in the service of an individual's self-interest. It does not follow that 'sharing expectations' promotes 'collaborative problem-solving': the sharing *may* promote collaboration *or* dissent, unity *or* competition. The dramaturgical model holds nothing more than that changes in relationships may occur by encouraging the actors to pay attention to their strategic interactions; the consequence of such attention may be that more energy is devoted to more effective dissimulation, or to more openness. Machiavelli's activities as a change agent are readily explained by this model, as are those of Carl Rogers or Abraham Maslow. Thus changes in relationships may arise collaboratively or they may arise from the advocacy of particular interests, as exemplified by the work of Schmuck and Miles (1971), for whom organizational development in schools is:

'. . . centrally a matter of clarifying and strengthening expressions of the conflicting interests of diverse groups, and of radically redistributing decision-making prerogatives so that low power groups can have more influence over an organization's fate . . . those low-power clients who are usually somehow allotted the back seat in education.'

The dramaturgical model, in and of itself, makes no normative assumptions about how actors *ought* to relate to each other nor about the normative methodology for effecting change beyond that which holds that in the final analysis some degree of mutual accommodation is necessary for the realization of individual goals and some degree of communication is necessary to the achievement of this accommodation.

The model assumes that differences are inevitable and are enforced by differing interpretations, that processes of collaboration (however temporary) and competition (however covert) do occur, and that coercion, dialogue, and negotiation may exist side by side within the same situational script. It makes no assumption concerning the desirability of particular processes of script mainten-ance beyond asserting that low attachment to roles may result in the eventual abandonment of them. It holds that the interventionist can come between these processes, can loosen the attachment of actors to parts and to scripts, and, thus, can provide the actor or actors with the opportunity to exercise choice. The interventionist himself exercises choice as to who to work with; he can select those with low power, the bit players, or those with high power, the stars. His client can be the Prince, the populace, or the proletariat. Or all of them.

The Power and Skills of the Interventionist

The interventionist also exercises some degree of choice as to the kind of script he encourages the actors to elaborate. If he believes in autonomy and self-actualization he will inevitably be involved in a different kind of script elaboration or construction to the consultant who believes in placing pro-ductivity before people. If his interpretation of the workplace script is that it would benefit from an infusion of humanitarian thinking, it is this aspect that he will stress; if he considers that concern for people can be allied with concern for productivity he will contribute this to the emerging script, and so on. As a professional dramaturg he is in a powerful position to affect more than the outlines of the play and the performances of the actors. Thus he may start with the microsociological processes of face-to-face interaction, but he is aware and may ensure that his social actors are aware that no lasting change will occur in the performance unless the scenery and the props are brought into line with the new script. Less metaphorically, although according centrality to the interpretation and performances of social actors, the dramaturg does not forget the technology, nor the environment within which the elements of organizing are to occur.

However much the actors may want to put on a different show they may not have the resources to stage it. Again as Kaufman (1971) puts it: '. . . resource limitations commonly bind organizations fixedly to their established repertoires of behaviour'.

The actor's and the interventionist's interpretation of these resource limitations (and technological constraints) enter into the construction of new scripts. It may be easier to overcome and test the limitations of human performance ('He will not want to talk about that', 'I'll be thought stupid if I raise that') than it is to confront and overcome perceived technological and resource limitations to change. Indeed the latter may not be capable of resolution.

It is clear from the previous chapters, and from the discussion so far in this one, that the interventionist both as critic and dramaturg is in a position to exercise considerable influence. In many ways he is a pivotal or central figure; not only can he choose the actors with whom he works but he also has the opportunity of having some of his own lines written into the script. Some interventionists may eschew this opportunity, claiming that their role is merely to facilitate the process of rewriting and rehearsing the new parts; others may seize upon it and virtually rewrite the entire situational script themselves. A not inconsiderable amount of traditional consultancy is based upon the attempted imposition of scripts; much of the intervention carried out in the emerging organization development tradition purports to be of a less imposing variety. It is frequently claimed by interventionists of this persuasion that script imposition is bound to fail since it is likely to be resisted by the social actors subjected to it. Conversely, scripts which have been evolved by the actors are much more likely to receive more than temporary performance since the actors involved in them have been instrumental in the elaboration of the lines and the parts. Thus they own what they perform; in the language of the theatre they have an interest in the play.

The activities of the interventionist, even in circumstances where he does not impose the script or perhaps particularly in such circumstances, are crucial to the outcome. Both in his activities as a critic and as a dramaturg, his interpretations and his repertoire of skills will influence the nature of the metatheatrical perspective he invites the actors to adopt. The interventionist, as I have stressed, does not come naked to the conference table, even the non-directive helper, the so-called client-centred consultant, is in the business of influencing others. He is concerned to express dramaturgically (i.e. through his performance) to his client that he has respect for him, that he can empathize with his circumstances, and that he is a genuine caring person. It is, in my opinion, impossible to conceive of an intervention process in which the interventionist exerts no social influence. If he is not to be simply in the business of substituting one imposed script for another he must so behave as to reduce this possibility. If, that is, he believes in humanistic values, his behaviour must embody them. He must neither cast others into roles they do not wish to assume nor, if he wishes the social actors to achieve a metatheatrical perspective, must be become caught up in the prevailing situational scripts. His intervention, therefore, calls for certain attributes and the deployment of considerable skills.

The question of attributes I will consider later; for the moment I wish to draw attention to the skills the dramaturgical model implies are necessary to effective intervention.

Clearly the interventionist as critic must exercise considerable diagnostic skills. At the minimum he is required to become familiar with the situational scripts which surround them. He may acquire this familiarity through asking the social actors (whose attachment may, however, preclude an awareness of the scripts); he may simply observe performances paying attention to what is said, by whom, to whom, and with what consequences, and to what messages appear to be transacted by the actors' tone of voice, their postures, their expressions, their gestures, and their silences. He may apprehend the full impact of particular situational scripts by experiencing them himself and having to disengage from them. Whatever way he comes to an awareness of the scripts I believe it important that he himself at this stage assumes the role of observer and sympathetic explorer of issues rather than is cast into or assumes an expert stance. His behaviour should be such as to cast others into behaving 'normally', performing their scripts with little regard for him. During interviews his altercasting and self-presentation should be such as to facilitate the clients exposition and exploration of issues. Such behaviour is facilitated by the skills of the consultant in displaying empathy, showing that he is able to come close to seeing things the way that the client sees them—showing, that is, that he can accurately take the role of the other, displaying overtly the mental processes of interpretation and reflecting to the client what he takes the client to be saying. Rather than *assuming* that he understands what the client is saying he tests his understanding openly with the client. Thus he ensures as far as possible that he is not making premature and inaccurate interpretations but, more importantly, he communicates to the client that he is listening and is able to apprehend the client's frame of reference.

In exploring potentially threatening areas, such as the degree of attachment the actor has for a particular part or situational script, I believe that the interventionist needs to go beyond simply attending to what is being said to him. He needs to communicate to the client—the actors to whom he is talking—that he can be trusted, that he has some concern for them as individuals, and that he will not use the information they impart in a destructive or irresponsible fashion. He can, of course, declare this, but his declaration must be reinforced by his performance. He must display genuineness and respect in working with the client if he is to be allowed to enter fully into his world (Carkuff, 1969, Egan, 1975).

In claiming that the effective interventionist must display genuineness I am advocating strategic interaction on the part of the interventionist. In order to have the client respond openly and honestly, the interventionist presents himself as genuine and a person who respects the client. There appears to be something of a contradiction about the idea of genuineness being performed. Genuineness is often thought of as a moral quality, not an assumption based upon a set of activities. I do not believe that the contradiction is real in that, as I have indicated, the actor is often constrained to *be* the parts that he plays; the interventionist *is* genuine or, if he is not, is displaying the behaviour which normally warrants such an assumption with sufficient skill to convince the client. Either way he successfully casts the client into responding in the manner he desires. Thus interventionists can *be* genuine or can effectively perform as though they were genuine (as can con-men, magicians, stage actors, and so on). The essence is that they succeed by their spontaneity, non-defensiveness, consistency, and humanness in conveying a quality of trustworthiness to the client which leads him to explore issues he may otherwise not have explored.

The conveying of respect also functions in the same way to cast the client into the role of being forthcoming. Egan (1975), whose extension of Carkuff's ideas is extremely valuable, notes that 'Respect is communicated principally by the way the helper *orients himself toward* and *works with the client*'. Again this is a skill and like the communication of genuineness can be learned. The effective interventionist communicates by his behaviour that he is willing to work with the client, that he regards him as worth the investment of time and effort, that he has concern for the unique qualities that constitute the client, and that he expects the client to be self-determining. Each and every message conveys to the client that he is respected by the consultant and contributes to a less defensive exploration of the client's performances.

Thus the interventionist's performance contributes to the gathering of data for his subsequent review of the situational scripts which constitute the organization (or that part of it with which he is concerned). The quality of that data has much to do with his skill. Assume for the moment, opposite conditions: that the activity of the interventionist as an observer has been clumsy and intrusive and that he has conveyed in his interactions that he is not much concerned about these particular social actors and has conveyed that what they are jointly enacting is the product of some form of mental aberration. The subsequent attempts to feedback data, by such an interventionist, I would none too humbly suggest, are unlikely to meet with success.

Thus, in the diagnostic or review stage, the skills of the interventionist are deployed so as to generate what Argyris terms 'valid information'. In the process of collecting these data, but more particularly in the process of sifting, the interventionist's interpretations become important features. The data are organized, are structured, and are put in a form which reflect the values and ideas the interventionist brings to the situation. It is impossible to make a neutral presentation; the interventionist has attended to certain features of the interaction and has ignored others. His predispositions have entered into the review and coloured it.

Not only has the interventionist influenced the decision as to who should provide data and to whom it should be fed back; he also clearly influences the nature of the feedback. An interventionist in the Blake and Mouton tradition will feed back different data to one in the Argyris tradition; Lawrence and Lorsch pay attention to some issues, Fritz Steele to others. Interventionists as dramaturgs may share a number of common values, but the scripts they put forward for consideration may vary considerably.

As dramaturg, the interventionist displays a number of skills over and beyond those already discussed. He displays empathy, genuineness, respect, and is clearly attending to what is being said and done, but he is also engaging in confronting behaviour, supportive behaviour, and straightforward script-rewriting behaviour.

As a confronter, the interventionist no longer passively accepts with unconditional regard the discrepancies and distortions which appear from time to time in the performances and accounts he is privy to. Instead he challenges them and seeks to draw the attention of the actors to them in order to 'develop the kind of self-understanding that leads to constructive behavioural change' (Egan, 1975). The feedback of the data itself and the construction the interventionist puts upon it is often confronting, and may bring about the situation where the client says, in effect, 'Now I can see what we are up to and how self-defeating (destructive, ineffective, etc.) it is.' In my experience many feedback sessions have this quality of revelation which I term, irreverently, the 'road-to-Damascus' effect.

Some, however, do not have this quality; the data are rejected or the defensiveness of the actors is such that no thorough discussion of them can occur. In such circumstances the interventionist's skills in effectively alienating them from their parts, in making the familiar strange in a way in which it is not overpoweringly threatening, are at a premium. Such is the meaning of confrontation as used in this context: a responsible attempt to reveal to the client not only the nature of the situational scripts he participates in but also the nature of the ploys and strategies he utilizes to justify his lack of examination of these scripts. The goals of confrontation are to help the actors explore areas of feelings, experiences, and performances that they have been reluctant to explore, to help them understand the consequences of their performances, and, finally, to help them learn how to adopt a confronting or metatheatrical perspective for themselves.

To bring about this exploration and learning, the interventionists must employ a judicious mix of confronting and supporting behaviour. Too much confrontation, too sharp an encounter with threatening material, may bring about a retreat; too much support may lead to a cosy collusion to avoid any meaningful exploration.

Above all the interventionist as dramaturg must be adept at offering some alternative frames of reference to his clients. It is not enough that he brings about a high degree of awareness through his reasons, analyses, disengagements, confrontations, and so on. Indeed the anguish of the actors may well be sharpened once they are able to achieve the metatheatrical perspective. In such circumstances social actors may be completely at a loss to know what to do other than that which was brought them to their present circumstance. It is not sufficient to know that one is behaving ineffectively, not sufficient to struggle and strive to come to this state of holy awareness. Insight without the possibility of resolution of the issues one is now privy to is not usually welcomed. The interventionist must be able to offer (or at least have the skills to work with the client to develop) an alternative interpretation, an alternative script, and series of parts. The objective is an alteration in the persisting identity of the relationships that have been subjected to review and confrontation. Without this feedback is not worth a candle and may even be an irresponsible activity.

Thus the interventionist is a powerful figure, a fully fledged man of the theatre of social life, not a literary hack hired to botch up and doctor a creaking vehicle for an ageing star.

The skills outlined above are in short supply; nor, in my opinion, are they easily required. It is a matter of regret that the heavy emphasis that organization development practitioners place upon participation and democracy has led to a belief that almost any one, genius, fool, or charlatan, can become an effective interventionist. The becoming modesty of Argyris, Blake, Beckhard, Bennis *et al.* effectively conceals the high level of skill and charisma needed to do the kind of work that they do. Their evident star quality must facilitate their acceptance in the performances they are called upon to criticize and rewrite. Just as in the theatre there are a few key directors so in organization development there are a few key interventionists, and it does no one any good pretending otherwise. Failure to acknowledge the crucial centrality of the interventionist and the dependence of the social actors upon him as they struggle to come to terms with their personal and situational scripts leads directly to the circumstance which I believe characterizes the field at the moment: too many amateur dramatics and not enough professional theatre. In the theatre the director has a key role to play just as in the revision of situational scripts the interventionist has a key role. It is not a place for amateurs and the unskilled, however well intentioned they may be.

Some Further Implications of the Dramaturgical Perspective

Two or three other points seem to arise from the ideas I have outlined in these pages. First it takes a long time to get a new show on the road. I know it is a basic law of organization development that it is long term, but I feel the need to reiterate the amount of time and energy it takes to bring about changes in relationships. In my estimation it can take a year or so to effectively change one situational script; attempts to change the scripts which hold together entire organizations or communities in my opinion are quite misguided (including, of course, my own). It follows that since the resources to work simultaneously on several scripts are not likely to be available, the interventionist must choose carefully which scripts are crucial. In many cases, therefore, it is sensible to begin at the top since, presumably, that is where many of the key decisions are made. However, it could be important in some circumstances to concentrate on budgetting scripts, planning scripts, or relations-with-the-unions scripts. Whatever the script it is essential that all of the social actors involved recognize that simply becoming aware of the problem of past scripts and the potential delights of revised scripts is not enough. The approach I am advocating is based upon classical rather than method principles of acting. I do not consider it responsible nor even interesting to loose the social actor upon a rough and ready new script to scratch and mumble his way through. Having identified a new part for himself the actor must be helped to build that part, step by step, gesture by gesture, line by line. Failure so to do I believe, leads directly to the retreat into old scripts at the first sign of difficulty with the inchoate new script. It is very difficult to change scripts and nothing is gained by pretending otherwise or, still worse, pretending it is all up to the actors.

A further implication is that much of organization development practice has been and will no doubt continue to be of a conservative nature. Since a great deal of the work is either explicitly or implicitly based upon systems theory it is hardly surprising that this should be the case. Even where this is less obviously the case the conservatism is still present. The interpretations a particular interventionist brings to an organization or group may be many and varied. Tannenbaum and Davis (1969) note a set of shared values that are perhaps 'the most pervasive common characteristic among people in laboratory training and in organizational development work', and I would not quarrel with the listing. The values they indicate are essentially humanistic ones, but even so, perhaps surprisingly, they see no inconsistency between the propagation of these values and the acceptance of entities such as large-scale corporations. Indeed they argue that 'Growing evidence suggests that humanistic values not only resonate with an increasing number of people in today's world, but are also highly consistent with the effective functioning of organizations built on the newer organic model'. Thus for many if not all organization development practitioners there is no necessary conflict between the pursuit of individual happiness or self-fulfilment and the performance of a task.

Few, very few, interventionists would disagree with this taken-for-granted interpretation of the purpose of intervention: to promote the best fit between the need to perform tasks and the need for self-actualization. It is, I would argue, a central and unquestioned feature of most, if not all, interventions. Very few interventionists look upon organizations as entities which must be destroyed, even fewer still challenge the ideas of property and capitalism which inform the structure and practice of much of Western industrial production. Hardly any theorists or practitioners declare that they wish to see the abolition of the managerial class and the installation of workers' control and none, to the best of my knowledge, have advocated 'creative anarchy' as the appropriate form of organization development.

I note these points to establish that however humanistic the world views imparted by the interventionist, with the emphasis upon positive evaluation of individuals, self-development, expression of feelings, authentic behaviour, avoidance of gamesmanship, trust, confrontation, collaboration, and so on, the overall thrust of his interpretations is likely to be as conservative as that of the senior managers with whom he works. Most of these interpretations arise within and sustain the prevailing socioeconomic system.

Whatever the reputation organization development theorists and practitioners may have attributed to them for radical perspectives on organizational life, their basic interpretations about behaviour in organizations are rarely radical. Most of them take for granted, and would be appalled if it were to be seen that they were threatening, the socioeconomic base of the present structure of things.

Nonetheless, there is room, I believe, for the avant-garde as well as the commercial theatre; perhaps we who pride ourselves on our ability to stand aside from scripts should take some of our own advice and ask ourselves more often whether or not we are really contributing by not challenging more forcefully and radically the prevailing socioeconomic scripts within which we apply our skills. Perhaps we should offer our services more often to the underprivileged and the disadvantaged, the weak and the unorganized, rather than spending so much time, as many of us do, on behalf of the systems, helping people adjust to their organizations.

Conclusion

I began this book by proclaiming that the prevailing theories were not appropriate to the development of the practice of changing social relationships within organizations. I have suggested that the way forward lies neither in the utilization of technological nor organic metaphors but in the consideration of face-to-face interaction as made up of scripts and performances.

The body of appropriate knowledge is as yet sparse, little more than a lean and hungry frame in need of fattening and fleshing out. I make no claim that the foregoing pages have added an ounce of flesh to that body; as I indicated that was not my purpose. What I hope to have achieved is to have raised a nagging doubt which causes practitioners to consider whether or not in their practice they ought to consider issues of scripts and strategies, players and performers, heroes, heroines, villains, and fools.

References

Adler, A. (1956), in Preface to H. L. Ansbacher (Ed.), *The Individual Psychology of Alfred Adler*, Basic Books, New York.

Alderfer, C. P. (1976), Change processes in organizations, in M. Dunnette (Ed.), *Handbook of Industrial and Organizational Psychology*, Rand-McNally, Chicago.

Allport, G. W. (1960), The open system in personality theory, *Journal of Abnormal and Social Psychology*, **61**, 307–311.

Ansbacher, H. L. (1971), Alfred Adler and humanistic psychology, *Journal of Humanistic Psychology*, **1**, 53–63.

Argyris, C. (1954), *Integrating the Individual and the Organization*, John Wiley and sons, New York.

Argyris, C. (1970), *Intervention Theory and Method*, Addison-Wesley, Reading, Mass.

Argyris, C. (1971), *Management and Organization Development*, McGraw-Hill, New York.

Argyris, C. (1973), *On Organizations of the Future*, Sage Publications, Beverly Hills, Calif.

Argyris, C. (1974), *Behind the Front Page*, Jossey Bass, San Francisco, Calif.

Ashby, W. Ross (1956), *An Introduction to Cybernetics*, Chapman and Hall, London.

Ball, D. W. (1972), The definition of the situation: some theoretical and methodological consequences of taking W. I. Thomas seriously, *Journal for the Theory of Social Behaviour*, **2**(1), 61–82.

Bavelas, A. (1960), Leadership: man and function. *Administrative Science Quarterly*, **1**(4) 491–498.

Beckett, S. (1956), *Waiting for Godot*, Faber, London.

Beckhard, R. (1969), *Organization Development: Strategies and Models*, Addison-Wesley, Reading, Mass.

Beier, E. G. (1966), *The Silent Language of Psychotherapy*, Aldine, Chicago.

Benne, K. D., and Sheats, P., Functional Roles and Group Membership, *Journal of Social Issues*, **4**(2), 41–49.

Bennis, W., Benne, K. D., and Chin, R. (1969), *The Planning of Change*, 2nd ed., Holt Rinehart and Winston, New York.

Berger, P. (1963), *Invitation to Sociology*, Penguin, London.

Berger, P., and Luckmann, T. (1966), *The Social Construction of Reality*, Doubleday and Co., New York.

Berger, P., and Pullsberg, S. (1966), Reification and the sociological critique of consciousness, *New Left Review*, **35**(1), 56–71.

Berne, E. (1964), *Games People Play*, Deutsch, London.

Bertalanffy, L. von (1962), General systems theory—a critical review, *General Systems*, **VII**, 1–20.

Biddle, B. J., and Thomas, E. J. (1966), *Role Theory: Concepts and Research*, John Wiley and Sons, New York.

Blake, R. R., and Mouton, J. S. (1969), *Building a Dynamic Corporation Through Grid Organization Development*, Addison-Wesley, Reading, Mass.

Blau, P., and Scott, W. R. (1963), *Formal Organizations: A Comparative Approach*, Routledge and Kegan Paul, London.

Blumer, H. (1969), *Symbolic Interactionism*, Prentice-Hall, Englewood Cliffs, N.J.

Brecht, B. (1940), *Kurze Beschriebung einer Neuem Technik der Schauspielkunst, die einen Verfremdungseffekt Hervorbringt*, Versuche, Frankfurt.

Brown, G. (1972), *In My Way*, Penguin, London.

Buckley, W. (1967), *Sociology and Modern Systems Theory*, Prentice-Hall, Englewood Cliffs, N.J.

Buckley, W. (1968), *Modern Systems Research for the Behavioural Scientist*, Aldine, Chicago.

Buhler, C., and Allen, M. (1972), *An Introduction to Humanistic Psychology*, Brooks/Cole, Monterey, Calif.

Burke, K. (1966), *A Grammar of Motives and a Rhetoric of Motives*, Meridian/World Publishing, Cleveland and New York.

Carkuff, R. R. (1969), *Helping and Human Relations*, Vols. I and II, Holt Rinehart and Winston, New York.

Carlson, S. (1951), *Executive Behaviour: A Study of the Work Load and the Working Methods of Managing Directors*, Strombergs, Stockholm.

Cooley, C. H. (1964), *Human Nature and the Social Order*, Scribner, New York.

Daix, P. (1965), *Picasso*, Thames and Hudson, London.

D'Aprix, R. M. (1972), *Struggle for Identity*, Dow Jones-Irwin Inc., Homewood, Ill.

Dalton, G. W. (1970), in Negandhi and Schwitter (Eds.) *Influence and Organizational Change in Organization Behaviour Models*, Comparative Administration Research Institute, Kent, Ohio.

Dalton, G. W. (1970), Influence and Organizational Change, in Negandi, A. R. (Ed.) *Modern Organization Theory*, Kent State University Press, Ohio.

Dayal, I., and Thomas, J. M. (1968), Operation KPE: developing a new organization, *Journal of Applied Behavioural Science*, **4**(4), 473–506.

Drucker, P. (1954), *The Practice of Management*, Harper and Row, New York.

Duncan, H. D. (1968), *Symbols in Society*, Oxford University Press, New York.

Durkheim, E. (1938), *The Rules of Sociological Method*, University of Chicago Press, Chicago.

Egan, G. (1975), *The Skilled Helper*, Brooks/Cole, Monterey, Calif.

Fink, S. L., Beak, J., and Taddeo, K. (1971), Organization, crisis and change, *Journal of Applied Behavioural Science*, **71**, 15–37.

French, W. L., and Bell, C. H. (1973), *Organization Development*, Prentice-Hall, Englewood Cliffs, N.J.

Friedman, G. (1961) *The Anatomy of Work: The Implications of Specialization*, Ind ed., Heinemann, London.

Gergen, K. J. (1971), *The Concept of Self*, Holt Rinehart and Winston, New York.

Goffman, E. (1959), *The Presentation of Self in Everyday Life*, Doubleday, Garden City. N.Y.

Goffman, E. (1961), *Encounters*, Bobbs-Merrill, Indianapolis.

Goffman, E. (1969), *Strategic Interaction*, Basil Blackwell, Oxford.

Goldschmidt, W. (1972), An ethnography of encounters, *Current Anthropology*, **13**, 59–78.

Golembiewski, R. (1972), *Renewing Organizations*, F. E. Peacock, Itasca, Ill.

Goodenough, W. H. (1974), On cultural theory, *Science*, **186**, 435–436.

Greenfield, T. Barr (1973), Organizations as social inventions: rethinking assumptions about change, *Journal of Applied Behavioural Science*, **9**(5), 551–574.

Gross, N., Mason, W., and McEarhern, A. W. (1958), *Explorations in Role Analysis: Studies of the School Superintendency Role*, John Wiley and Sons, New York.

Gurwitsch, A. (1966), *Alfred Schutz: Collected Papers*, Vol. III, Martinus Nivhoff, The Hague.

Harre, R. (1974), Some Remarks on 'Rule' as a Scientific Concept in Mischel, T. (Ed.), *Understanding Other Persons*, Blackwell, Oxford.

Harrison, R. (1972), Role Negotiation: A Tough Minded Approach to Team Development in Burke, W., and Hornstein, H. *the Social Technology of Organization Development*, N.T.L. Learning Resources, Washington, D.C.

Herberg, W. (1956), *The Writings of Martin Buber*, Meridian Books, New York.

Holthusen, H. E. (1961), Brecht's Dramatic Theory in Demetz, P. (Ed.) *Brecht*, Prentice-Hall, Englewood Cliffs, N.J.

Hunt, R. (1974), *Interpersonal Strategies for System Management: Applications of Counselling and Participative Principles*, Brooks/Cole, Monterey, Calif.

Johnson, H. M. (1960), *Sociology: A Systematic Introduction*, Harcourt Brace and Company, New York.

Kahn, R. L. (1974), Organization development: some problems and proposals, *Journal of Applied Behavioural Science*, **10**(4), 485–502.

Kahn, R. L., Wolfe, D. M., Quinn, R. P., Snoek, J. D., and Rosenthal, R. A. (1964), *Organizational Stress: Studies in Role Conflict and Ambiguity*, John Wiley and Sons, New York.

Katz, D., and Kahn, R. L. (1966), *The Social Psychology of Organizations*, John Wiley and Sons, New York.

Kaufman, H. (1971), *The Limits of Organizational Change*, University of Alabama Press, Ala.

Kelly, G. A. (1970), A Brief Introduction to Personal Construct Theory in Bannister, D. (Ed.) *Perspectives in Personal Construct Theory*, Academic Press, New York.

Kuriloff, A. H. (1972), *Organizational Development for Survival*, American Management Association, New York.

Laing, R. D. (1969), *Self and Others*, Penguin, London.

Langer, J. (1969), *Theories of Development*, Holt Rinehart and Winston, New York.

Lawrence, P. R., and Lorsch, J. W. (1969), *Developing Organizations: Diagnosis and Action*, Addison-Wesley, Reading, Mass.

Levinson, H. (1972), *Organizational Diagnosis*, Harvard University Press, Cambridge, Mass.

Lippit, G. L. (1971a), *Organization Renewal*, Appleton-Century-Crofts, New York.

Lippit, G. L. (1974b), *Visualizing Change*, N.T.L. Learning Resources, Fairfax, Va.

Lofland, J. (1976), *Doing Social Life*, John Wiley and Sons, New York.

Lyman, S. M., and Scott, M. B. (1975), *The Drama of Social Reality*, Oxford University Press, New York.

McCall, G. J., and Simmons, J. L. (1966), *Identities and Interactions*, Free Press, New York.

McGregor, D. (1960), *The Human Side of the Enterprise*, McGraw-Hill, New York.

McHugh, P. (1958), *Defining the Situation*, Bobs-Merrill, Indianapolis and New York.

Mangham, I. L. (1977), Definitions, interactions and disengagement: notes towards a theory of intervention processes in T-groups, *Journal of Small Group Behaviour*, **8**(4), 487–510.

Marcel, G. (1960), *The Mystery of Being*, Gateway, Chicago.

Margulies, N., and Raia, A. P. (1972), *Organization Development: Values, Process and Technology*, McGraw-Hill, New York.

Marrow, A. J., Bowers, D. G., and Seashore, S. E. (1967), *Management by Participation*, Harper and Row, New York.

Martin, M. (1956), Differential decisions in the management of an industrial plant, *Journal of Business*, **29**, 250–261.

Maslow, A. (1970), *Motivation and Personality*, rev. ed., Harper and Brothers, New York.

Maslow, A. (1971), *The Farther Reaches of Human Nature*, Viking Press, New York.

Matson, F. W. (1969), What ever became of the third force?, *American Association of Humanistic Psychology Newsletter*, **6**(1), 14–15.

Matson, F. W. (1971), Humanistic theory: the third revolution in psychology, *The Humanist*, **2**, 7–11.

Mead, G. H. (1966), *The Social Psychology of George Herbert Mead*, University of Chicago Press, Chicago.

Mead, G. H. (1964), *Selected Writings*, Bobbs-Merrill, Indianapolis and New York.

Melly, G. (1965), *Owing Up*, Penguin, London.

Meltzer, B. N. Petras, J. W., and Reynolds, L. T. (1975), *Symbolic Interactionism: Genesis, Varieties and Criticism*, Routledge and Kegan Paul, London.

Melville, H. (1948), *Moby Dick: or The Whale*, Scribners, New York.

Miles, R. E. (1975), *Theories of Management: Implications for Organizational Behaviour and Development*, McGraw-Hill, New York.

Mintzberg, H. (1973), *The Nature of Managerial Work*, Harper and Row, New York.

Moore, W. E. (1962), *The Conduct of the Corporation*, Random House, New York.

Morrison, E. E. (1966), *Men, Machines and Modern Times*, M.I.T. Press, Cambridge, Mass.

Nisbet, R. A. (1969), *Social Change and History*, Oxford University Press, London.

Nisbet, R. A. (1972), *Social Change*, Basil Blackwell, Oxford.

Nobbs, D. (1976), *The Fall and Rise of Reginald Perrin*, Penguin, London.

Nord, W. (1974), The failure of current applied behavioural science: a marxian perspective, *Journal of Applied Behavioural Science*, **10**(4), 557–578.

Pages, M. (1974), An interview with Max Pages—N.Tichy, *Journal of Applied Behavioural Science*, **10**(1), 8–26.

Park, R. E. (1927), Human nature and collective behaviour, *American Journal of Sociology*, **32**, 738–739.

Parsons, T. (1937), *The Structure of Social Action*, McGraw-Hill, New York.

Pepper, S. C. (1942), *World Hypotheses*, University of California Press, Berkeley, Calif.

Perinbanayagam, R. S. (1974), The definition of the situation: an analysis of the ethnomethodological and dramaturgical view, *Sociological Quarterly*, **15**, 521–541.

Perrow, C. (1972), *Complex Organizations*, Scott Foresman, Glenview, Ill.

Reason, P. (1976), *Notes on Holistic Research Processes and Social System Change*, Working Paper, Centre for the Study of Organizational Change and Development, University of Bath.

Reisman, D. (1953), *The Lonely Crowd*, Yale University Press, Yale.

Righter, A. (1962), *Shakespeare and the Idea of the Play*, Penguin, London.

Robertson, T. W. (1956), Caste, in Rowell, G. (Ed.), *Victorian Melodramas*, Oxford University Press, London (1956).

Rogers, C. R. (1961), *On Becoming a Person*, Houghton Mifflin, Boston, Mass.

Sapir, E. (1968), Communication, in D. G. Mandelbaum (Ed.), *Selected Writings of Edward Sapir*, University of California, Berkeley and Loss Angeles.

Schank, R., and Abelson, R. (1977), *Scripts, Plans, Goals and Understanding*, Lawrence Erlbaum Associates, Hillsdale, N.J.

Schein, E. H. (1966), *Organizational Psychology*, Prentice Hall, New Jersey.

Schein, E. H. (1969), *Process Consultation: Its Role in Organization Development*, Addison-Wesley, Reading, Mass.

Schmuck, R., and Miles, M. B. (1971), *Organization Development in Schools*, National Press, Palo Alto, Calif.

Schutz, A. (1962), *Collected Papers*, Vol. I, Martinus Mijhoff, The Hague.

Schutz, A. (1967), *The Phenomenology of the Social World*, Heinemann, London.

Sherwood, J. J., and Glidewell, J. C. (1975), Planned Renegotiation: A Norm-Setting OD Intervention in Burke, W. (Ed.), *New Technologies in Organization Development*, University Associates, La Jolla, Calif. (1975).

Silverman, D. (1970), *The Theory of Organizations*, Heinemann, London.

Simmel, G. (1950), in K. Wolff (Ed.), *The Sociology of George Simmel*, Free Press, New York.

Solomon, L. N. (1971), Humanism and the training of applied behavioural scientists, *Journal of Applied Behavioural Science*, 7(5), 531–547.

Stanislavsky, C. (1950), *Building a Character*, Elek Books, London.

Stebbins, R. A. (1969), Studying the definition of the situation: theory and field research strategies, *Canadian Review of Sociology and Anthropology*, 6(4), 114–132.

Steele, F. (1973), *Physical Settings and Organization Development*, Addison-Wesley, Reading, Mass.

Strauss, G. (1976), Organization development, in Dubin, R. (Ed.) *Handbook of Work, Organization and Society*, Free Press, New York.

Styan, J. L. (1963), *The Elements of Drama*, Cambridge University Press, London.

Swanson, G. (1965), On explanations of social interaction, *Sociometry*, 28, 101–123.

Tannenbaum, R., and Davis, S. A. (1969), Values man and organizations, *Industrial Management Review*, 10(2), 67–86.

Taylor, F. (1911), *The Principles of Scientific Management*, Harper and Brothers, New York.

Thomas, W. I. (1923), *The Unadjusted Girl*, Little Brown and Co., Boston, Mass.

Thompson, J. D. (1967), *Organizations in Action*, McGraw-Hill, New York.

Tuman, M. (1973), *Patterns of Society*, Little Brown and Co. Boston, Mass.

Turner, R. H. (1962), Role Taking: Process Versus Confirmity in Rose. M. (Ed.), *Behaviour and Social Processes*, Routledge and Kegan Paul, London.

Wagner, H. R. (1973), The Scope of Phenomenological Sociology: Considerations and Suggestions in Pasthas, G. (Ed.), *Pehnomenological Sociology*, John Wiley and Sons, New York.

Watzlowick, P., Weakland, J. H., and Fisch, R. (1974), *Change*, Norton and Co., New York.

Weber, M. (1947), *The Theory of Economic and Social Organization*, Free Press, New York.

Weick, K. (1969), *The Social Psychology of Organizing*, Addison-Wesley, Reading, Mass.

Weinstein, E. A. (1969), The Development of Interpersonal Competence in Goslin, P. (Ed.), *Handbook of Socialization Theory and Research*, Rand-McNally, Chicago, Ill.

Weinstein, E. A., and Deuschberger, P. (1964), Tasks, bargains and identities in social interaction, *Social Forces*, 42, 451–456.

Weisbord, M. R. (1974), The gap between OD practice and theory—and publication, *Journal of Applied Behavioural Science*, 10(4), 476–484.

Wenburg, J., and Wilmot, W. (1973), *The Personal Communication Process*, John Wiley and Sons, New York.

Wesker, A. (1960), *Roots*, Penguin, London.

Westlake, D. (1966), *The spy in the ointment*, Random House, New York.

Willet, J. (1964), *Brecht on Theatre*, Methuen, London.

Winn, A. (1971), Reflexions sur la strategie du T-group et le role d'agent de changement dans le development organizationnel, *Bulletin de Psychologie*, 25, 296, 250–256.

Wrong, D. (1961), The oversocialized conception of man in modern sociology, *American Sociological Review*, XXVI, 183–193.

Index

148